ZILLI
light

ZILLI
light

photography by Steve Lee

SIMON & SCHUSTER

A CBS COMPANY

Love and thanks to my publishers for making this possible, especially during the recession;
also my agents Fiona and Mary for getting me the deal. To my PA Luisa, for coping with my scribbles and for
helping to test the recipes. To my beautiful family – Nikki, my wife, for putting up with me while I was
writing at home and for having to look after our children, Rocco and Twiggy, alone.
But most important, thank you to all my fans and customers for buying this book.
Love you all!

First published in Great Britain by Simon & Schuster UK Ltd. 2010.

A CBS Company Simon & Schuster UK Ltd, 1st Floor, 222 Gray's Inn Rd, London WC1X 8HB. www.simonandschuster.co.uk

Managing Editor: Heather Bateman *Editor:* Nicole Foster *Design:* Jane Humphrey

Photography: Steve Lee *Home Economist:* Karen Taylor *Stylist:* Jo Harris *Photography Assistant:* Douglas Lee

1 3 5 7 9 10 8 6 4 2 Colour Reproduction by Dot Gradations Ltd, UK. Printed and bound in China ISBN 978-1-84737-556-8

CONTENTS

When I first came up with the title for this book all I was thinking about was the Celebrity Fit Club TV programme that I took part in a few years ago. It proved, literally, to be a totally life-changing experience. **For me it was the start of a new lifestyle and a new way of looking at food** – the focus of my cooking altered, with new ingredients and different patterns of eating.

When I agreed to take part in the programme I was ready for a change. I knew that it might be an idea to ditch smoking, to cut down on drinking. The motivation to go down that route came from my own family history. Too many of my close relations had died young, of heart disease. I needed to give myself a chance.

At the time I went on the programme, although I'm a chef, I wasn't really thinking about what I was eating – the sort of food or the quantity. Running my restaurants, food was always there, necessary fuel, and I grabbed a bite when I could. The usual routine was to share a pasta meal with my staff mid-morning, before we opened for lunch. Then I was cooking, and, necessarily, tasting everything, constantly. I was actually eating a lot without noticing. And exercise didn't feature at all – my priority in getting to work was to grab a parking spot as near the restaurant as possible.

While on the TV programme the rules were strict: I was allowed to eat small portions of fish or meat, and salads; there were to be no carbs or alcohol for a month. After that I was allowed pasta once a week, in the evening as long as I was exercising the following morning, otherwise at lunchtime. I took the regime seriously, I started to exercise, and the result was that I lost 3 stone in as many months. But, more importantly, I felt great.

So how are things now? Well, OK, I've regained a bit of weight, but I'm comfortable with that. I'm not adhering to anything like such a strict diet but I'm following the basic guidelines. I eat pasta twice a week, I've drastically reduced my caffeine intake, I've cut down on carbs and I go for brown bread and rice. I haven't stopped exercising.

I sometimes have to force myself to keep up the routine but I do get to the gym three times a week for cardiovascular workouts: running, cycling, rowing and swimming.

And I now cycle to work every day – 30 minutes each way. I definitely still feel great.

I am particularly proud of this book, which is a true reflection of me, now, at fifty-three years old. The recipes are influenced by my Italian tradition but with my own take. There is much from my great Mediterranean diet, which, with its balance of oils, red wine, fish and vegetables, is definitely the healthiest alternative, and I have taken the opportunity to pass on other things that I've picked up along the way. There are lots of tips I could share but the most important are: only eat when you are hungry; remember to keep it small, light and often (five small meals a day); eat oily fish three times a week; try not to eat fruit after your evening meal (it stops the digestive system working properly). And – the last one – don't eat late at night. Have a light evening meal, then go to bed two or three hours later. I promise you'll sleep better, and will wake properly re-energized.

Keep in mind that the last meal of the day should be light and healthy – a fist-size portion of protein and vegetables. Breakfast is important too – I go for wholegrain cereal with fruit and yogurt. You can eat most at lunchtime, which again is the classic Mediterranean way. If you want to indulge a little this is the best time to do it. If you can't resist dessert, it can happen at lunchtime. Forget about snacks between meals. You don't need them on this sort of diet; you'll be so full of energy you won't crave that afternoon sugar fix.

We're not talking calorie-counting here, though if you're following that sort of diet many of the recipes, especially in the fish section, can easily be adapted. Whatever the reason you bought this book, please try and use it to its full potential. Switch off 'auto-pilot' and be prepared to change your routine and move out of the comfort zone of the familiar. It really is worth taking the trouble to look after yourself – you'll find that taking care of your kids or whoever you're responsible for will follow easily.

I hope you enjoy this book as much as I enjoyed writing it! 'Always remember losing weight is a marathon not a sprint' Buon appetito!

Aldo's tips:

- Only eat when you are hungry
- Eat small, light and often
- Try not to eat fruit after your evening meal
- Don't eat late at night
- Eat oily fish three times a week
- Check that all seafood is sustainable, by looking for the Marine Stewardship Council's blue label

SALADS

...& dressings

The great thing about salads is that they can be used as snacks; prepare them in advance – without the dressing – and, when you feel yourself craving a quick fix, you can reach for one of these lovely salads rather than a chocolate bar.

The salads here are some of the most exciting dishes in the book. Salad is such a versatile option, from the spice of Spicy Crab Salad (see page 22) to the coolness of Caprese Salad (see page 23). The sheer variety of salad leaves, dressings and vegetables can be overwhelming, but I have managed to focus on my real favourites, particularly Wild Leaf & Herb Salad (see page 21), which is exquisite. Herbs are often thought of as an accompaniment to cooking rather than celebrated in their own right; a pity as they are delicious served with just lemon juice and oil.

The great thing about these salads is that they can be used as snacks; prepare them in advance so that when you feel yourself craving a quick fix, you can reach for one of these lovely salads rather than a chocolate bar. **Remember to watch your portions and dressings – these should be light and low in fat.**

I think escarole, watercress and rocket make for the best salad bases as they are packed with flavour. But let your imagination run wild and add whatever ingredients you prefer.

A couple of the salads contain fruit – apples and pears are fantastic in salad. As always try to make sure the fruit is seasonal whenever possible.

Aldo's tips:

- Prepare salads in advance, keeping the dressing aside until the last minute
- If you're craving a quick fix, reach for a salad instead of a chocolate bar
- Keep portions light
- Keep dressings light and low
- Use salads as snacks
- Mix and match recipes to suit your desires

This salad gives a great protein boost and makes an excellent light lunch. Add some basil or your favourite herb to give it another dimension.

lentil, feta & roasted pepper salad

Serves 4

Preparation time: 15 minutes

Cooking time: 15 minutes

3 x 400 g cans lentils

2 red peppers

2 yellow peppers

200 g feta cheese, cut into cubes

a handful of rocket, roughly chopped

1 tablespoon extra virgin olive oil

salt and freshly ground black pepper

Drain the lentils and wash thoroughly.

Put the whole peppers on a baking tray and place under a hot grill for 15 minutes, turning occasionally, until charred. Remove and place in a bowl, cover with clingfilm and leave to cool.

Once the peppers have cooled, remove the skin and seeds and roughly chop. Place in a salad bowl with the lentils, feta, rocket and olive oil. Season, toss gently and serve.

...& light meals

Keep starters light; they are supposed to whet your appetite, not satiate it completely. In a restaurant, don't binge on the free bread or you can be full before the first course arrives!

This is definitely my favourite course of any meal – it sets the tone for what's to come – and you are often very hungry by the time you sit down to it! My advice with starters is to always keep them light; they are supposed to whet your appetite, not satiate it completely.

My other tip, when dining out in restaurants, is to actually wait for the starter and not binge on the free bread on offer – many times in the past, out for a meal with friends, we've eaten so much bread we're full before the first course arrives!

The starters I have chosen in this chapter can all be adapted into a light supper – so please don't be too prescriptive about their place in the order of a meal. Mix and match these recipes to suit your needs. You'll notice the ever-present Mediterranean influence, from the oily fish to the delicious vegetables, such as aubergines and artichokes. These are the flavours that remind me of home.

Wherever possible, buy vegetables when they are in season. Not only will they taste better, they will be cheaper, too. Seasonality is an essential part of the Mediterranean diet, and that is something I want to promote in this book.

So the key to these starters is lightness and freshness – go easy on the dressing and the portions, and you won't go wrong. Personally, I think my simple Marinated Sardines with Extra Virgin Olive Oil, Garlic & Chilli (see page 54) cannot be beaten – the taste of summer on a plate!

Aldo's tips:

- Keep starters light; they are supposed to whet the appetite, not slate it
- Go easy on dressings and portions
- In a restaurant, wait for the starter to arrive and don't binge on bread
- Adapt these starters to make a light supper
- Mix and match recipes to suit your needs

The sweetness of the peas works really well with the scallops for a great-tasting dish. If you like you can leave out the pancetta and just add some mixed leaves with a lemon dressing instead.

pan-fried scallops with pea purée & crispy pancetta

Serves 4

Preparation time: 5 minutes

Cooking time: 7 minutes

4 slices pancetta

1 teaspoon sea salt

12 scallops, cleaned, without roes

Pea purée

450 g peas (defrosted if frozen)

a handful of mint leaves

salt and freshly ground black pepper

To make the pea purée, place the peas and mint in a blender and blitz. Put in a small saucepan and heat gently. Season.

Arrange the pancetta slices in a baking tray and cook under a hot grill until crispy. Remove and set on kitchen paper to drain.

Meanwhile, heat a griddle pan on top of the stove. When it is very hot, sprinkle with the sea salt then sear the scallops – 1 minute each side and they will be ready. The salt prevents the fish from sticking to the pan.

Put three spoonfuls of pea purée on each plate, place a scallop on each heap of purée and top the serving with a slice of crispy pancetta. Serve immediately.

One of my favourite breakfast dishes, but in my fish restaurant this is a big hit as a starter. It's easy to prepare and really tasty.

pepper & chilli smoked mackerel with poached egg

Serves 4

Preparation time: 10 minutes

Cooking time: 4 minutes

3 tablespoons extra virgin olive oil

4 pepper and chilli smoked mackerel
     fillets (about 175 g each)

juice of ½ lemon

350 g mixed salad leaves, washed

salt and freshly ground black pepper

4 poached eggs

1 tablespoon chopped fresh parsley

Heat 2 tablespoons olive oil in a frying pan and add the mackerel. Fry for 2 minutes each side until warmed through. Remove.

Mix the remaining olive oil with the lemon juice and dress the salad leaves. Season.

Serve the warm mackerel on the salad, topped with a poached egg and decorated with parsley.

Tuna doesn't need a lot of cooking and it's great raw, Japanese-style, with some sushi rice, but this is my Italian version – so go for it.

seared tuna carpaccio with paprika & rocket

Serves 4
Preparation time: 10 minutes
Cooking time: 3 minutes

1 small tuna fillet (about 600 g)
salt
2 tablespoons freshly cracked black
     pepper
3 teaspoons paprika
4 tablespoons olive oil
juice of 1 lemon
3 tablespoons extra virgin olive oil
freshly ground black pepper
a handful of rocket

Season the tuna fillet with ½ teaspoon salt, the cracked pepper and paprika. Heat a frying pan and add the olive oil. Place the tuna in the pan, sear for 1 minute each side then remove from the pan and leave to cool.

Whisk the lemon juice with the extra virgin oil and add some salt and freshly ground black pepper. Pour half over the rocket and toss.

Slice the cooled tuna very thinly and arrange on a flat plate. Place a handful of the dressed rocket in the middle, drizzle with more lemon oil and serve.

When in season, asparagus is great with salty Parma ham and cheese – a fantastic combo for any time of day.

asparagus in parma ham gratin on a bed of rocket

Serves 4

Preparation time: 20 minutes

Cooking time: 10 minutes

16 large asparagus spears

8 slices Parma ham

25 g butter, softened

25 g Parmesan cheese, grated

freshly ground black pepper

2 tablespoons olive oil

4 tablespoons balsamic vinegar

75 g bag of rocket

Prepare the asparagus by peeling the stalks and removing the hard lower part, about 2.5 cm.

Bring a large shallow pan of water to a steady simmer. Add the asparagus and simmer for 4 minutes until bright green and just tender. Drain and set aside to cool slightly.

Wrap two asparagus spears in each slice of Parma ham and place on a foil-lined grill tray.

Mix the butter and Parmesan cheese and season with black pepper. Dot the Parmesan mixture all over the wrapped asparagus then grill under a hot grill for 4 minutes, until the cheese is bubbling.

Mix the olive oil and balsamic vinegar and use half to dress the rocket. Arrange the salad in the centre of four serving plates then top each with two bundles of asparagus. Drizzle the remaining dressing around the salad.

This recipe screams summer in Italy. Watermelon when in season and ripe is hard to beat – grilled with pineapple it is just fantastic. The escarole leaves give a slightly bitter, peppery flavour. You could also add some blue cheese to this salad. Fab!

grilled watermelon salad with walnuts, pineapple & broad beans

Serves 4

Preparation time: 10 minutes

Cooking time: 2 minutes

½ watermelon, deseeded and cut
    into large chunks

2 slices pineapple, cut into large
    chunks

300 g broad beans, blanched and
    skins removed

80 g shelled walnuts

1 bunch fresh mint, roughly chopped

300 g baby spinach

2 tablespoons extra virgin olive oil

2 red endives, leaves separated

1 escarole, leaves torn

Heat a griddle pan or barbecue and chargrill the pieces of watermelon and pineapple for 1 minute on each side. Remove from the pan and toss with all the remaining ingredients.

Arrange the tossed watermelon salad in the middle of individual serving plates.

Well, what can I say about this recipe? Couscous takes no time to prepare and you could grill the vegetables the day before, to make a quick easy meal.

grilled vegetables & couscous

Serves 4

Preparation time: 10 minutes

Cooking time: 10 minutes

1 aubergine

2 courgettes

1 red pepper, deseeded and cut
   in four

1 yellow pepper, deseeded and cut
   in four

3 tablespoons extra virgin olive oil

salt and freshly ground black pepper

200 g couscous

450 ml hot chicken or vegetable
   stock

50 g butter

2 tablespoons chopped fresh mint

1 tablespoon chopped fresh
   coriander

juice of 1 lemon

Cut the aubergine and courgettes into 1 cm slices. In a large bowl, combine the aubergine, courgettes, peppers, olive oil, salt and pepper. Mix well.

Heat a griddle pan and cook the vegetables for 4 minutes on each side, until marked and cooked through.

Place the couscous in a bowl, add the stock, cover and leave for 5 minutes. Separate the grains with a fork then add the butter, herbs and lemon juice and season.

Mix together the couscous and vegetables and serve.

Trout is generally underrated as a fish, but if you fancy a quick snack or light lunch, this is the recipe for you. Smoked salmon could be used as an alternative.

smoked trout & potato salad

Serves 4

Preparation time: 20 minutes

Cooking time: 10 minutes

500 g unpeeled waxy potatoes

100 ml extra virgin olive oil

50 ml lemon juice

1 tablespoon red wine vinegar

1 garlic clove, crushed with sea salt

freshly ground black pepper

2 tablespoons chopped fresh mint

2 tablespoons chopped fresh parsley

2 tablespoons finely sliced spring
  onions

1 celery stalk, diced

1 tablespoon capers

1 red pepper, deseeded and sliced
  thinly

250 g smoked rainbow trout, skin
  and bones removed

Lemon mayonnaise

1 egg yolk

50 ml lemon juice

grated zest of 1 lemon

sea salt and freshly ground black
  pepper

100 ml mild olive oil

To make the lemon mayonnaise, place the egg yolk, lemon juice and zest, sea salt and pepper in a bowl or food processor and whisk until combined. Add the oil drop by drop, whisking constantly. Once it starts to thicken, add the oil in a steady stream until fully combined. If the mayonnaise looks too thick, add a tablespoon of warm water. Keep in the fridge.

Cook the potatoes in salted water until tender. Drain and allow to cool for a few minutes or until you can handle them, before peeling and slicing.

Place the olive oil, lemon juice, vinegar, crushed garlic and sea salt and pepper in a bowl and whisk. Stir in the herbs, spring onions, celery, capers and red pepper.

Add the potatoes to the dressing while they are still warm and stir gently to combine.

Divide the potato salad between serving plates and top with flakes of the smoked trout. Drizzle with the lemon mayonnaise.

I love mackerel done in any way – baked, roasted, marinated with Japanese mirin – but this recipe really works well on delivering great flavours.

mackerel fillet 'sandwiches' & gremolata

Serves 4
Preparation time: 15 minutes (plus marinating)
Cooking time: 30 minutes

8 fresh medium mackerel fillets,
    scaled
1 tablespoon extra virgin olive oil
sea salt and freshly ground black
    pepper

Gremolata
5 tablespoons extra virgin olive oil
grated zest and juice of 2 lemons
3 garlic cloves, finely chopped
7 tablespoons finely chopped
    fresh parsley
2 tablespoons finely chopped
    rosemary

To make the gremolata, mix all the ingredients together and leave to marinate for 30 minutes.

Preheat the oven to 180°C/fan oven 160°C/Gas Mark 4.

Using a teaspoon, spread a quarter of the gremolata over the flesh side of one of the mackerel fillets then place another fillet on top (to make a 'sandwich'). Repeat with the remaining mackerel fillets. Place the mackerel sandwiches on a baking tray, drizzle over a little olive oil and season. Cook in the oven for 30 minutes.

This is a classic Italian starter and can be found in lots of Italian restaurants. Make sure you choose a prime cut of beef, such as fillet. The truffle oil also serves to make this a real luxury starter.

rare beef with rocket & truffle oil

Serves 4

Preparation/Cooking time: 10 minutes

450 g lean beef fillet

2 tablespoons salt

4 tablespoons freshly ground black
   pepper

2 tablespoons extra virgin olive oil

8 tablespoons chopped rocket

juice of 1 lemon

1 tablespoon truffle oil

100 g Parmesan cheese shavings

Season the beef with half the salt and pepper. Add the olive oil to a frying pan and heat. When very hot, add the beef fillet and sear on all sides (roughly 1 minute each side). Allow to cool slightly.

Using a sharp, thin-bladed knife, finely slice the beef and arrange on a large plate. Place the rocket on top.

Mix the remaining salt and pepper with the lemon juice and truffle oil then drizzle over the rocket and meat. Sprinkle with Parmesan shavings and serve.

Unlike tuna, salmon is quite cheap and readily available. You can buy wild salmon in season but organic farmed salmon is available all year and is just as good. Lime is used in many of the recipes in this book – its flavour adds a fantastic zing to the food.

salmon carpaccio with fennel

Serves 4

Preparation time: 40 minutes (plus chilling)

500 g sashimi/sushi-grade salmon

1 tablespoon extra virgin olive oil

1 tablespoon lime juice

2 tablespoons soy sauce

1 tablespoon chopped fresh dill

1 tablespoon chopped fresh coriander

salt and freshly ground black pepper

1 fennel bulb, thinly sliced

½ medium cucumber, thinly sliced

1 tablespoon sesame seeds, toasted

2 tablespoons finely chopped spring
   onions

grated zest of 1 lime

Wrap the salmon in clingfilm and freeze it for 20–30 minutes until the fish is partly frozen; this will make it easier to slice. Remove the salmon from the freezer and unwrap. Using a sharp knife or a slicer, cut across the grain into thin slices. Arrange the salmon slices around a large platter.

Whisk together the oil, lime juice, soy sauce, dill and coriander. Season to taste. Toss the fennel slices in some of the dressing and place in the middle of the salmon. Arrange the cucumber slices over the salmon, then sprinkle with the sesame seeds, spring onions and lime zest and drizzle with more dressing. Leave in the fridge for 1 hour before serving.

You should eat oily fish at least three times a week, so this recipe is great as it can be kept in the fridge for up to two weeks – as long as the sardines are completely covered in oil. Alternatively, eat it sooner and reuse the marinade for another batch of fish.

marinated sardines with extra virgin olive oil, garlic & chilli

Serves 4

Preparation time: 10 minutes (plus marinating)

12 fresh small sardines, boned

500 ml bottle white wine vinegar

juice of 1 lemon

5 tablespoons sea salt

4 bay leaves

5 garlic cloves

3 tablespoons whole peppercorns

To finish

3 garlic cloves, finely chopped

2 chillies, deseeded and finely chopped

2 tablespoons finely chopped fresh parsley

75 ml extra virgin olive oil

Place the sardines in a flat dish and cover with the rest of the ingredients. Leave to marinate in a cool place for at least 12 hours.

To finish, remove the sardines from the marinade and dip in a bowl of water. Pat dry with a kitchen cloth and place on a shallow plate. Sprinkle with the garlic, chilli and parsley and pour over the olive oil – make sure the fish is completely covered with the oil. Marinate for at least 3 hours before serving.

Figs are great with dolcelatte, Gorgonzola or Stilton. Be sure not to overcook the figs and serve this dish hot, as the cheese should be just melting.

baked figs with dolcelatte

Serves 4

Preparation time: 10 minutes

Cooking time: 12 minutes

8 firm ripe figs

80 g dolcelatte cheese

8 fresh basil leaves

salt and freshly ground black pepper

3 tablespoons extra virgin olive oil

150 g baby spinach

1 teaspoon balsamic vinegar

Preheat the oven to 180°C/fan oven 160°C/Gas Mark 4.

Cut a cross in the top of each of the figs without cutting through them completely. Put a teaspoon of the dolcelatte and a basil leaf in each fig. Place the figs in an ovenproof dish, season with salt and pepper and drizzle with 2 tablespoons of the olive oil.

Bake in the oven for 12 minutes, until the figs are soft and the cheese has melted.

Toss together the spinach, remaining oil and balsamic vinegar. Serve the figs on top of the spinach salad.

This wonderful fish is from the same family as mackerel and sardines. It is so affordable and cooks in no time.

stuffed herrings with garlic & chilli sauce

Serves 4

Preparation time: 25 minutes

Cooking time: 30 minutes

12 fresh herrings, scaled and heads
   removed
1 tablespoon olive oil
1 onion, finely chopped
1 garlic clove, part-crushed
75 g fresh breadcrumbs
1 tablespoon grated Parmesan
   cheese
2 tablespoons chopped fresh parsley
1 egg yolk
40 g smoked mozzarella cheese,
   finely diced
juice of 3 lemons
salt and freshly ground black pepper
lemon wedges and fresh parsley,
   to garnish

Garlic & chilli sauce

2 garlic cloves, finely chopped
1 chilli, deseeded and chopped
4 tablespoons olive oil

Preheat the oven to 180°C/fan oven 160°C/Gas Mark 4.

Fillet the herrings, leaving them whole (or ask your fishmonger to do this for you) and clean the insides.

Heat the oil in a medium saucepan and fry the onion with the part-crushed garlic clove over a low heat until softened, approximately 5 minutes. Discard the garlic clove.

Remove the pan from the heat and stir in the breadcrumbs, Parmesan, chopped parsley, egg yolk and mozzarella. Mix in the juice of two of the lemons and season to taste.

Using a teaspoon, fill the inside of the herrings with the stuffing and arrange them in a greased ovenproof dish. Pour over the remaining lemon juice, cover with foil and bake in the oven for 30 minutes.

Meanwhile, make the garlic and chilli sauce. Cook the garlic and chilli in the olive oil over a medium heat for 15 minutes.

Remove the herrings from the oven and place on a serving plate. Pour over the garlic and chilli sauce and garnish with lemon wedges and fresh parsley. Serve immediately.

Aubergine is not used very much in this country; in Italy it is a king and we use it for baking, dips, ratatouille – everything! Try this recipe to appreciate the versatility of this vegetable.

aubergine **bruschetta**

Serves 4
Preparation time: 10 minutes (plus salting and marinating)
Cooking time: 8 minutes

2 aubergines, sliced
sea salt and freshly ground black
** pepper**
2 garlic cloves, finely chopped
100 ml extra virgin olive oil
juice of 1 lemon
2 tablespoons chopped fresh mint
8 slices ciabatta bread

Place the sliced aubergines in a colander and sprinkle with sea salt to remove excess water. Leave for 2 hours.

Grill the aubergine slices on a barbecue or in a griddle pan until well marked on each side, about 2 minutes per side.

Mix together the garlic, oil, lemon juice and mint. Season. Put the cooked aubergine slices in a bowl and pour over the marinade. Leave for 1 hour, stirring occasionally.

Toast the ciabatta. Place the aubergine on top of the toasted bread, spoon over any remaining marinade and serve immediately.

A frittata is an open omelette. You can make this with pretty much any vegetables you like; you could even sprinkle some soft cheese on top, making a great family feast for hardly any money at all.

courgette & artichoke **frittata**

Serves 4
Preparation time: 10 minutes
Cooking time: 22 minutes

2 tablespoons extra virgin olive oil
1 onion, finely sliced
200 g can artichokes, drained and
    quartered
200 g courgettes, diced
175 g fresh broad beans, blanched
    and skins removed
6 eggs
2 tablespoons chopped fresh parsley
45 g pecorino cheese, grated
salt and freshly ground black pepper

Heat the oil in a large frying pan and cook the onion for 8 minutes over a low heat. Add the artichoke quarters and courgettes and cook for a further 2 minutes before adding the broad beans.

Beat together the eggs, parsley and pecorino, and season. Pour into the frying pan and cook over a low heat for 10 minutes, shaking the pan often to make sure the frittata doesn't stick. Place under a hot grill for 2 minutes to finish the cooking. Allow to cool slightly before serving.

PASTA

Aim to keep pasta portions to 100 grams or so, and keep sauces really light. You want the ingredients to speak for themselves not to be smothered with a thick sauce.

Where would I be without this chapter? Like Sophia Loren's infamous quote, I too owe everything to pasta. It shaped my cooking career from the earliest stage and was the first thing my mother taught me to make, at the age of eight. Now I love to make pasta at home with my little son, Rocco. You should give it a go, it's good fun and the results are delicious. See the recipe for Basic White Pasta Dough on page 198.

The way pasta is eaten in the UK is entirely different from the way we eat it in Italy. Spaghetti Bolognese bears no resemblance to our Italian dish, which we serve with shell-like pasta or macaroni. Italians never include cream in a carbonara sauce and the size of the servings here is staggering; in Italy pasta is simply one course of many. My pasta dishes are authentic and served in the style and quantity you would find in any Italian home or restaurant.

Aim to keep portions to 100 grams or so, and keep sauces light; you want the ingredients to speak for themselves not to be smothered with a thick sauce. Personally, I love nothing more than a simple *aglio e olio* – garlic, chilli and extra virgin olive oil – cheap, quick and delicious. And always add pasta to the sauce, never the other way round.

These days I love eating pasta with fish and fish sauces. It's also a great way to get your children started on fish – you can hide it in a tomato sauce. Again, be mindful of seasonality – why use canned tomatoes in the summer, when you have gorgeous fresh ones at your disposal?

Wherever possible, try to eat pasta at lunchtime rather than in the evening, and limit your intake to three times a week. Similarly for the pizza options – they make excellent light suppers but keep them for once in a while rather than every night. One of the best ways to eat pizza is to create a very thin crust and cover the lovely hot base with raw ingredients such as buffalo mozzarella, plum tomatoes, basil, rocket and extra virgin olive oil. Delicious!

Aldo's tips:
- **Keep pasta portions small, about 100g**
- **Keep sauces light**
- **Always add pasta to the sauce, never the other way round**
- **Eat pasta at lunchtime rather than in the evening**
- **Limit pasta to three times a week**
- **Try fish in pasta sauce to get children started on fish**
- **Keep pizza crusts thin**
- **Eat pizza at lunchtime and only once in a while at night**

Duck is not usually served as a pasta sauce, but once you try this you will become addicted.

tagliatelle with duck ragout & pecorino

Serves 4

Preparation time: 30 minutes

Cooking time: 1 hour 10 minutes

1 duck

60 ml olive oil

2 small onions, sliced

1 carrot, sliced

2 garlic cloves, chopped

2 celery stalks, sliced

¼ bottle good red wine

200 ml meat or vegetable stock

900 g passata

2 rosemary sprigs

2 thyme sprigs

2 bay leaves

1 whole chilli

salt and freshly ground black pepper

400 g tagliatelle

200 g pecorino cheese, grated

Quarter the duck and then cut into smaller pieces. Remove some of the fat but leave the skin on. Heat the oil in a large pan and brown the pieces of duck at a high heat, skin-side down.

Reduce the heat and add the onions, carrot, garlic and celery to the pan. Fry gently until browned. Pour in the wine and simmer until the liquid has evaporated. Add the stock and passata.

Strip the leaves from the rosemary and thyme sprigs and add to the pan together with the bay leaves and whole chilli. Cover with a tight-fitting lid and simmer for approximately 1 hour. Season to taste.

Bring a large saucepan of salted water to the boil. Add the pasta and cook for 6–8 minutes, or according to the packet instructions, until al dente. Drain.

Remove the duck from the pan and place in a serving dish. Discard the whole chilli. Add the pasta to the remaining sauce and cook for a further minute, tossing occasionally to ensure the pasta is well coated.

Serve the tagliatelle and sauce in a separate dish from the duck, sprinkled with some pecorino. Serve the duck with a green vegetable, such as spinach or broccoli.

Bolognese is normally associated with beef, but pork was actually the favourite in my family. Minced pork is lighter than beef and, I think, makes a tastier sauce.

gluten-free pasta with pork bolognese

Serves 4

Preparation time: 15 minutes

Cooking time: 1 hour 20 minutes

2 tablespoons olive oil

40 g butter

1 onion, finely chopped

1 celery stalk, trimmed and finely
     chopped

1 carrot, finely diced

250 g lean pork mince

200 ml full-bodied red wine, such as
     Montepulciano D'Abruzzo

400 g can chopped tomatoes

salt and freshly ground black pepper

2 tablespoons chopped fresh
     flat-leaf parsley

350 g gluten-free tagliatelle or
     other pasta

freshly grated Parmesan cheese,
     to serve

Heat the oil and butter in a large deep pan, add the onion, celery and carrot and stir well. Cook over a gentle heat for 5 minutes until just beginning to soften.

Increase the heat, add the mince and cook for 10 minutes, stirring constantly for the first 3 minutes to break up all the lumps. Pour in the red wine and simmer for 3 minutes. Stir in the tomatoes and season well. Partially cover the pan and cook over a low heat for 1 hour, until the meat and vegetables are very tender and the juices thickened, stirring occasionally during cooking. Add the parsley.

During the final 20 minutes of cooking the sauce, bring a large pan of salted water to the boil. Add the pasta, stir and return to a gently rolling boil. Cook according to the packet instructions until al dente. Drain.

Add the pasta to the bolognese sauce and mix well. Cook for a further minute, then serve in deep bowls with a sprinkling of Parmesan.

I had never experimented with gluten-free pasta until my wife Nikki became wheat intolerant. I had to find a solution because she loves pasta. So this recipe was created – it is now on my menu at Zilli Fish and the customers love both this and a variation we serve using crayfish. The sauce works just as well without the pasta: you can eat it as it is or serve it with some gnocchi. It reminds me of my childhood, when my mother used to cook it all the time.

gluten-free pasta with monkfish & squid

Serves 4
Preparation time: 15 minutes
Cooking time: 15 minutes

1 tablespoon extra virgin olive oil
8 spring onions, finely sliced
½ red chilli, deseeded and finely
   chopped
1 garlic clove, part-crushed
100 g squid rings
350 g monkfish, cleaned and cut into
   chunks
175 ml dry white wine, such as
   Trebbiano
500 g jar passata
1 tablespoon chopped fresh basil
   leaves, plus extra basil leaves
   to garnish
sea salt flakes and freshly ground
   black pepper
350 g gluten-free linguine or other
   pasta

Heat the olive oil in a large saucepan and fry the spring onions, chilli and part-crushed garlic clove for 1 minute, then discard the garlic clove.

Add the squid and cook for 2 minutes, then add the monkfish chunks and fry for another 2 minutes. Pour in the white wine and let it bubble for 2 minutes. Add the passata and chopped basil and leave to cook for 3 minutes. Season with sea salt flakes and freshly ground black pepper.

Bring a large pan of salted water to the boil and add the pasta, gently easing it into the water. Stir and return to a rolling boil. Cook the pasta according to the packet instructions.

When the linguine is cooked, drain, reserving a little of the cooking water, and add to the saucepan with the sauce. Toss to combine. If the sauce is too thick, add some of the reserved pasta water.

Serve immediately, garnished with torn basil leaves.

This pancake version of lasagne is a lot lighter than the traditional version and it's not too difficult to make. Just use best-quality ingredients: organic eggs and free-range chicken.

pancake timballo with baby chicken balls

Serves 6–8

Preparation time: 20 minutes

Cooking time: 2 hours

Pancakes

2 medium eggs

300 ml milk

2 tablespoons sunflower oil

130 g plain flour

Chicken balls

500 g minced chicken

4 spring onions, finely chopped

2 garlic cloves, finely chopped

2 large shallots, finely chopped

1 long red chilli, deseeded and finely
  chopped

1 teaspoon dried oregano

2 tablespoons finely chopped fresh
  parsley

1 teaspoon finely chopped fresh
  basil

salt and freshly ground black pepper

2 egg yolks

100 g fine breadcrumbs

100 ml olive oil

To make the pancakes, mix the eggs, milk and half the oil in a jug. Sift the flour into a bowl and gradually beat in the egg mixture to make a smooth batter. Heat a 17.5 cm frying pan and wipe some of the oil over the base. Pour an eighth of the batter into the pan, swirling it around to spread it. Cook for 1–2 minutes until the batter is set and golden on the base. Flip over and cook for a further 1–2 minutes until golden on the other side. Repeat with the remaining mixture to make eight pancakes. Set aside.

To make the chicken balls, mix the chicken with the spring onions, garlic, shallots, chilli and dried and fresh herbs. Season, and mix in the egg yolks and half the breadcrumbs. Roll into small balls a little bigger than marbles, then roll in the remaining breadcrumbs until they are completely coated. Heat the olive oil in a frying pan and fry the chicken balls for about 3–4 minutes, until golden. Set aside.

Tomato sauce

1 tablespoon extra virgin olive oil

1 onion, finely chopped

1 garlic clove, finely chopped

2 x 500 g jars passata

Béchamel sauce

25 g unsalted butter

25 g flour

150 ml milk

beaten egg and freshly grated
Parmesan cheese, to finish

To make the tomato sauce, heat the oil in a frying pan, add the onion and garlic and cook for 3 minutes, until soft but not browned. Add the passata and simmer for 10 minutes, then add the chicken balls and cook for a further 10 minutes.

To make the béchamel, melt the butter in a small pan, add the flour, and cook for about 1 minute, stirring continuously. Add the milk a little at a time, stirring (or whisking) to ensure there are no lumps. Continue adding and stirring until you have made a smooth white sauce.

Preheat the oven to 180°C/fan oven 160°C/Gas Mark 4.

Spread some of the béchamel over the bottom of a medium-size baking tray. Cover with a layer of pancakes and then a layer of meatballs and sauce. Add some more béchamel, drizzle with beaten egg and sprinkle with Parmesan. Continue layering in this way, finishing with a layer of pancakes. Spread any remaining béchamel, beaten egg or tomato sauce over the top, sprinkle with grated Parmesan and bake for 30 minutes until bubbling and golden.

A fantastically versatile condiment, pesto is great to make yourself as it keeps for a long time and can be used with fish and meat as well as pasta. Always use a good-quality extra virgin olive oil.

trenette al pesto

Serves 4

Preparation time: 10 minutes

Cooking time: 10 minutes

200 g fresh basil

2 garlic cloves

20 g pine nuts, toasted

50 g Parmesan cheese, grated

50 g pecorino sweet sardo cheese, grated

30 g sun-dried tomatoes in oil

100 ml extra virgin olive oil

400 g trenette pasta

Wipe the basil leaves with a damp cloth and place in a mortar or food processor. Add the garlic, pine nuts, Parmesan, pecorino and sun-dried tomatoes and start to blend or pound with a pestle. Slowly add the olive oil and, with the machine running, if used, continue to blend until you achieve a paste.

Bring a large saucepan of salted water to the boil. Add the pasta and cook according to the packet instructions until al dente. Drain. Mix the pasta and pesto sauce together. Return the pan to the hob and heat quickly, then serve immediately.

Clams are great shellfish – the key here is not to cook them in wine as it changes the flavour, and fresh ingredients don't need much to bring out their flavours. Linguine would make a suitable alternative to fettuccine. Alternatively, leave out the pasta and eat these clams as a starter.

fettuccine **vongole**

Serves 4
Preparation time: 20 minutes (plus soaking)
Cooking time: 15 minutes

340 g clams
3 fat garlic cloves
4 tablespoons olive oil
1 red chilli
4 bay leaves
80 ml chicken stock
30 g fresh basil leaves
30 g fresh flat-leaf parsley, finely
  chopped
400 g fettuccine
extra virgin olive oil
salt and freshly ground black pepper

Soak the clams in salted water for 30 minutes to remove the grit, then wash in clean water and drain. Discard any clams that have opened.

Place the unpeeled garlic cloves on a clean surface and crush with the blade of a heavy knife. Put the oil in a large non-stick frying pan and add the garlic, chilli and bay leaves. Cook for 1 minute over a low heat. Add the clams, cover, and cook for 2–3 minutes until the clams have opened. Discard any clams that remain closed. Add the stock and simmer for 3 minutes over a medium heat. Add the basil and parsley and cook for a further 5 minutes over a low heat. Set aside.

Meanwhile, bring a large pan of salted water to the boil. Ease the pasta into the water and return to a rolling boil. Stir and cook for 5–8 minutes, or according to the packet instructions, until al dente. Drain.

Remove the whole chilli, garlic and bay leaves from the sauce and then toss the pasta with the clams. If you find there are too many shells, remove some. Drizzle with extra virgin olive oil and toss to mix. Adjust the seasoning and serve immediately.

This is a classic dish that all Italian restaurants were serving when I first came to England. I have tweaked it a bit so give it a try.

tagliatelle **carbonara**

Serves 4

Preparation time: 10 minutes

Cooking time: 10–12 minutes

100 g pancetta, rind removed and
　　cut into strips

400 g tagliatelle

8 egg yolks

50 g Parmesan cheese, finely grated

1 scant teaspoon freshly ground
　　black pepper

½ teaspoon freshly grated nutmeg

2 tablespoons chopped fresh parsley

Heat a large deep frying pan, add the pancetta and cook over a medium heat for 10 minutes until golden brown. There is no need to add any oil or butter as the pancetta will release its own fat.

Meanwhile, bring a large pan of salted water to the boil. Add the pasta and cook for 8–10 minutes, or according to the packet instructions, until al dente.

In a large bowl, mix together the egg yolks, Parmesan, pepper, nutmeg and parsley. Drain the pasta. Remove the bacon from the heat and add the pasta to the pan.

Add the pasta mixture to the egg mixture and toss. The heat from the bacon and pasta will cook the egg mixture. Serve immediately.

This very thin pasta absorbs more liquid than other pastas so make sure you don't serve it too dry. If you can't find smoked mozzarella, the normal sort will do.

angel-hair pasta with vegetables & scamorza

Serves 4
Preparation time: 15 minutes
Cooking time: 20 minutes

1 tablespoon extra virgin olive oil
50 g butter
1 onion, chopped
1 large carrot, finely sliced
1 celery stalk, finely sliced
1 red pepper, deseeded and finely
    sliced
1 yellow pepper, deseeded and
    finely sliced
sea salt flakes and freshly ground
    black pepper
150 g mascarpone cheese
400 g angel-hair pasta
½ vegetable stock cube
200 g scamorza (smoked mozzarella),
    thick rind removed and diced
extra virgin olive oil and balsamic
    vinegar, to serve

Heat the oil and butter in a large deep frying pan. Add the onion and cook for 5 minutes, until golden. Add all the vegetables and cook for 8–10 minutes on a slow heat, stirring frequently. Season well with sea salt and freshly ground black pepper. Stir in the mascarpone cheese and cook until melted.

Meanwhile, bring a large pan of salted water to the boil. Add the pasta to the boiling water once the vegetables are ready. Stir well with a large fork to separate the strands. Cook for 3 minutes, or according to the packet instructions, until al dente.

Drain the pasta, reserving 150 ml of the cooking water. Add the vegetable stock cube to the water and stir to dissolve. Add the pasta to the vegetables and toss well, using some of the reserved water to loosen the pasta.

Stir in the mozzarella, allowing it to melt. Adjust the seasoning if necessary. Divide the pasta between large bowls and drizzle with extra virgin olive oil and balsamic vinegar to serve.

Whether you are a vegetarian or not, you will love this dish. You can use frozen peas and beans out of season, making this a year-round favourite.

spaghetti with peas & broad beans

Serves 4

Preparation time: 15 minutes

Cooking time: 10 minutes

175 g fresh broad beans, shelled

175 g fresh peas, shelled

4 tablespoons olive oil

2 garlic cloves, finely chopped

½ red chilli, deseeded and finely
  chopped

2 tablespoons finely chopped fresh
  mint

juice of 1 lemon

salt and freshly ground black pepper

400 g spaghetti

freshly grated pecorino cheese,
  to serve

Bring a saucepan of salted water to the boil. Add the broad beans and peas and cook for 4 minutes. Drain well and remove skins from broad beans.

Heat the oil in a large frying pan and add the garlic and chilli. Cook over a low heat until the garlic is soft but not brown. Add the peas, broad beans, mint and lemon juice to the pan and cook for 1 minute. Season to taste.

Meanwhile, bring a large saucepan of salted water to the boil. Add the spaghetti and cook according to the packet instructions until al dente. Drain, reserving some of the cooking water.

Add the pasta and some of the cooking water to the vegetables and cook for a further minute. Serve immediately with some grated pecorino.

Many Sicilian recipes feature vegetables, especially aubergines, and spices, but this one adapts the classic Sicilian combination of anchovies and breadcrumbs for you to try something a bit different.

Sicilian-style spaghetti with tiger prawns

Serves 4
Preparation time: 10 minutes
Cooking time: 10 minutes

400 g spaghetti
3 tablespoons extra virgin olive oil
2 garlic cloves, finely chopped
30 g fresh anchovy fillets (or
    1 canned anchovy fillet), chopped
16 raw tiger prawns, heads
    removed, peeled and deveined
70 g breadcrumbs
2 tablespoons chopped fresh parsley
salt and freshly ground black pepper

Bring a large pan of salted water to the boil. Add the spaghetti and cook it according to the packet instructions until al dente. Drain, reserving 2 tablespoons of the cooking water.

Meanwhile, heat the olive oil in a frying pan. Add the garlic and anchovies and cook over a medium heat for about 1 minute. Add the tiger prawns and fry for a further 3 minutes, stirring constantly until the prawns are cooked. Stir in the breadcrumbs and turn off the heat. Add the parsley and season.

Add the drained pasta and 2 tablespoons cooking water to the tiger prawn pan and toss to combine. Serve immediately.

linguine with fresh crab

See recipe on next page.

The crab needs to be the best, so try to buy live crabs from a reliable fishmonger. *See photograph on previous page.*

linguine with fresh crab

Serves 4
Preparation time: 30 minutes
Cooking time: 15 minutes

4 whole crabs (800 – 900 g each)
1 leek, halved
fresh parsley sprigs, plus 1
    tablespoon finely chopped parsley
3 glasses white wine
5 whole garlic cloves and 3 garlic
    cloves, finely chopped
80 g pesto
4 tablespoons olive oil
1 teaspoon finely chopped chilli
4 courgettes, finely diced
400 g linguine

Put the crabs in a large saucepan with the leek, parsley sprigs, 2 glasses of wine, 5 whole garlic cloves and enough water to cover the crabs. Bring to the boil and cook for about 6 minutes.

Remove the crabs from the hot water and place immediately into iced water. When the crabs are cold, remove the meat from each. Open the head, remove all the brown meat and set aside. Remove the white meat from the legs but leave the claws. Mix the white and brown meat together. Crack the claws but leave whole. Place the claws in a baking dish, pour over the pesto and leave to marinate. Clean out the crab shells.

Preheat the oven to 200°C/fan oven 180°C/Gas Mark 6.

Heat the olive oil in a large saucepan, add the chopped garlic, chilli, brown and white crab meat, courgettes and chopped parsley. Fry for 1 minute then add the remaining wine. When the sauce has thickened, remove from the stove. Place the crab claws in the oven for 2 minutes.

Meanwhile, bring a large pan of salted water to the boil. Add the pasta and cook according to the packet instructions. When the pasta is cooked, drain and add to the sauce. Mix together and serve immediately. Present the dish with the linguine and sauce inside the crab shells and the crab claws placed on either side.

This is a very simple recipe that can be used for all sorts of fish or smoked salmon. If you can't find dill, fennel also works well.

pappardelle with salmon & dill

Serves 4
Preparation time: 10 minutes
Cooking time: 25 minutes

4 salmon fillets (about 160 g each)
salt and freshly ground black pepper
2 tablespoons chopped fresh dill
juice of 1 lemon
2 tablespoons olive oil
400 g pappardelle
2 garlic cloves, finely chopped
2 plum tomatoes, roughly chopped
200 g fresh spinach, chopped
1 tablespoon chopped fresh basil

Wash and prepare the salmon for cooking: season with salt and pepper and rub in the dill and lemon juice. Heat half the olive oil in a frying pan and fry the fish for 2 minutes each side, then flake into a bowl (the salmon should be rare).

Bring a large saucepan of salted water to the boil. Add the pasta and cook for 6–8 minutes, or according to the packet instructions, until al dente. Drain, reserving 2 tablespoons of the cooking water.

Heat the remaining olive oil in a saucepan, add the garlic and tomatoes and fry for 1 minute before adding the spinach and basil. Cook for another minute then add the cooked pasta and the 2 tablespoons cooking water. Stir in the salmon and cook for a further 2 minutes before serving.

Fresh tiger prawns are black in colour. Peel them and remove the heads, then use the shells to make a good fish stock.

pappardelle with tiger prawns
& vegetables

Serves 4

Preparation time: 20 minutes

Cooking time: 15 minutes

2 tablespoons vegetable oil

2 garlic cloves, finely chopped

1 red pepper, halved lengthways, deseeded and cut into long batons

1 yellow pepper, halved lengthways, deseeded and cut into long batons

1 courgette, trimmed and cut into matchsticks

75 ml white wine

400 g can whole peeled plum tomatoes

1 tablespoon olive oil

32–40 raw tiger prawns, heads removed, peeled and deveined

4–5 tablespoons fresh basil leaves

2 tablespoons chopped fresh flat-leaf parsley

salt and freshly ground black pepper

250 g pappardelle

Heat the vegetable oil in a large pan over a medium heat. Add the garlic and cook for 1 minute until golden brown. Stir in the red and yellow peppers and cook for a further 3–4 minutes. Stir in the courgette and cook for 1 minute more. Add the wine to the vegetables and bring to the boil. Cook for 3–4 minutes to evaporate the alcohol.

Place the tomatoes in a food processor and process until roughly chopped. Stir this purée into the vegetables and cook for 2 minutes.

Heat the olive oil in a small pan over a medium heat. Add the prawns and cook, stirring, for 1–2 minutes until heated through. Add the prawns, pan juices, basil and parsley to the tomato mixture. Season to taste.

Meanwhile, bring a large pan of salted water to the boil. Add the pasta and return to a rolling boil. Stir and cook for 5–7 minutes, or according to the packet instructions, until al dente. Drain, add to the vegetable and prawn mixture and toss well. Serve immediately with extra black pepper.

Mozzarella is the cheese that's always used in pizza, but try this vegetarian topping with goat's cheese. I personally love it as it gives a completely different flavour to the pizza. Thin-crust is what my son loves, so be guided by him and, if you make this for your kids, keep it nice and thin.

pizza with 3 toppings

Serves 4

Preparation time: 30 minutes (plus resting)

Cooking time: 20 minutes

500 g pizza dough (see page 200)

For vegetarians: Sun-dried tomato, goat's cheese & mushroom

3 tablespoons passata

125 g goat's cheese, diced

4 sun-dried tomatoes, finely chopped

10 mushrooms, thinly sliced

For children: Mozzarella, pepper, tomato & mushroom

3 tablespoons passata

125 g mozzarella cheese, grated

1 red pepper, deseeded and finely diced

4 tomatoes, cored and diced

10 mushrooms, thinly sliced

fresh basil, leaves torn

Healthy: Tricolore

125 g mozzarella, sliced

8 plum tomatoes, sliced

1 avocado, peeled, stoned and sliced

1 tablespoon extra virgin olive oil

1 rosemary sprig, leaves finely chopped

Preheat the oven to 180°C/fan oven 160°C/Gas Mark 4.

Divide the pizza dough into four and roll each piece into a thin 15–20 cm circle. Transfer to baking trays. You may need to work in batches. Spread the top of each pizza with passata, if used, and your choice of topping, and cook in the oven for 20 minutes.

For the classic Italian flag colours of the Tricolore; you could also add dried or semi-dried tomatoes for extra flavour. With this topping you don't need to spread passata on the base first.

To keep this dish light you need to make sure that the dough is very thin.
You can of course make small calzoni instead of one big one and eat them
as between-meal snacks.

calzone

Serves 2

Preparation time: 15 minutes

Cooking time: 20 minutes

cornmeal

½ quantity pizza dough (see
   page 200)

1 tablespoon extra virgin olive oil

170 g mozzarella, diced

2 slices Parma ham, cut into strips

salt and freshly ground black pepper

Preheat the oven to 230°C/fan oven 210°C/Gas Mark 8.
Lightly oil a baking tray and dust with the cornmeal.

On a floured surface, roll out the pizza dough to an
18 cm circle, then, using your hands and starting from
the middle, press outwards to form a 30 cm circle.
Place on the baking tray and brush with olive oil.

Scatter the mozzarella over one half of the pizza
leaving a 2 cm border around the edge. Lay the Parma
ham strips on top of the mozzarella and season.

Fold the other half of the base over the ham and
mozzarella to the other edge to make a semi-circle.
Roll the edges together firmly. Brush the calzone with
a little more oil then cook in the oven for 20 minutes.

There is something so satisfying about all bread-making. Once you have made this recipe you will want to make it again and again – the smell alone should make you happy.

focaccia

Makes 1 loaf
Preparation time: 20 minutes (plus proving)
Cooking time: 15 minutes

750 g strong white flour
1 teaspoon salt
20 g easy-blend yeast
90 ml melted margarine
450 ml lukewarm water
1 tablespoon extra virgin olive oil
sea salt flakes
4 cherry tomatoes, halved
2 garlic cloves, finely sliced
1 rosemary sprig, leaves roughly
**   chopped**

Sift the flour and salt into a large bowl and stir in the easy-blend yeast. Rub in 4 tablespoons melted margarine until the mixture resembles fine breadcrumbs then stir in the lukewarm water to form a rough dough.

Turn out the dough onto a well-floured surface and knead until it is smooth and springs back when gently pressed. Place in a lightly oiled bowl and cover with clingfilm. Leave in a warm place for 45 minutes to prove until almost doubled in size.

Preheat the oven to 220°C/fan oven 200°C/Gas Mark 7.

Gently knead the dough to knock back the air, then roll out into a 2 cm thick circle. Place on a large greased baking sheet and press down, using floured fingers, to make indentations at 2.5 cm intervals. Drizzle with the oil and sprinkle over the salt flakes, cherry tomatoes, garlic and rosemary.

Bake in the oven for 5 minutes, then reduce the temperature to 200°C/fan oven 180°C/Gas Mark 6 and cook for a further 10 minutes, until golden brown. Serve warm or cold.

RICE

...beans & grains

Grains and pulses add texture, colour and flavour to everything, from salads and soups to pastas.

The sheer variety of grains and pulses is phenomenal: from the fleshiness of the kidney bean to the tiny, jewel-like grains of quinoa, there is something for every taste and meal.

Grains and pulses add texture, colour and flavour to everything from salads and soups to pastas. They are generally cheap, have a long shelf-life and are very healthy.

The grains I have included in this chapter are all energy-boosting, fantastic for digestion and a great source of protein for those people who are keen to avoid animal proteins. I have included some more unusual grains such as spelt and quinoa, but you will find that most good supermarkets stock these now.

Rice is a versatile ingredient and if used the right way is also very healthy. If you are following a specific diet you could replace the white rice in these recipes with brown rice – generally speaking, it's better for you. Risotto is a staple of any Italian diet and I have included a few different options – the risotto with scallops is fit for a king.

Aldo's tips:

- Rice is versatile and healthy, if used the right way

  Grains and pulses:

- Add texture, colour and flavour to everything from salads and soups to pasta

- Are cheap and have a long shelf-life

- Can be energy-boosting

- Are fantastic for the digestion

- Are a good source of protein for non-meat eaters

Adding some chorizo would bring a zinging touch of chilli to this great winter-warming soup.

cannellini bean soup

Serves 6

Preparation time: 5 minutes

Cooking time: 20 minutes

1 onion, quartered

3 garlic cloves

40 g fresh parsley

2 tablespoons olive oil

2 x 400 g cans cannellini beans

1.2 litres chicken stock

salt and freshly ground black pepper

juice of 1 lemon

Blend the onion, garlic and parsley in a food processor until finely chopped.

Heat the oil in a pan, add mixture and cook until the onion is soft. Add the cannellini beans and cook for 2 minutes. Pour in the stock, season and bring to the boil. Cover and cook for 15 minutes until the beans are cooked.

Remove from the heat and mash with a fork. Add the lemon juice and reheat gently before serving.

This classic Italian vegetable soup doesn't normally include rice, but if you are trying to cut down the amount you eat my alternative version is a great filler.

minestrone of brown rice & vegetables

Serves 6
Preparation time: 20 minutes
Cooking time: 30 minutes

4 tablespoons extra virgin olive oil

50 g pancetta, diced

1 large onion, chopped

2 garlic cloves, finely chopped

100 g broccoli, cut into florets with stems peeled and chopped

2 medium carrots, diced

2 celery stalks, trimmed and diced

2 courgettes, diced

4 plum tomatoes, skinned, deseeded and diced

1.2 litres vegetable stock, made using 2 stock cubes

450 g fresh broad beans, shelled, or 300 g frozen broad beans

150 g brown rice

salt and freshly ground black pepper

40 g pecorino romano cheese

crusty Italian bread, to serve

Heat 2 tablespoons of the olive oil in a heavy pan and stir in the pancetta and onion. Cook over a low heat for 5 minutes until the onion is soft. Add the garlic, chopped broccoli stems and remaining vegetables apart from the broccoli florets and the beans. Fry for another 5–7 minutes, stirring frequently, until all the vegetables look bright in colour.

Pour in the stock and bring to the boil. Stir in the broad beans and rice and season. Simmer for 10 minutes; the rice should be just al dente.

Add the broccoli florets and cook for 5 minutes. Stir in the remaining olive oil and the pecorino cheese. Serve with crusty Italian bread.

Gnocchi is one of those dishes that has a reputation for being difficult to make, but you will see from this recipe that it is in fact very easy. My favourite way of serving gnocchi, particularly in the summer, is with green beans, pesto and some tomato concasse. Or try it with the Quick Tomato Pasta Sauce on page 199.

gnocchi

Serves 4
Preparation time: 10 minutes
Cooking time: 40 minutes

1 kg large floury potatoes, such as
   King Edwards
salt
2 egg yolks
200 g plain flour
1 litre chicken stock or water

Cook the unpeeled potatoes in a pan of boiling salted water for 30 minutes until soft. Drain and set aside until cool enough to handle.

Peel the potatoes and mash or press through a potato ricer into a bowl. Season with salt then beat the egg yolks and flour into the mashed potatoes, a little at a time. This will form a smooth, slightly sticky dough.

Tip the dough onto a well-floured board, then use your hands to roll it into long sausages about 1 cm thick. Cut into sections, each about 2 cm long. Place each piece on a fork and press down with your thumb, then roll onto the board, leaving grooves on one side of the gnocchi.

Bring the stock or water to the boil in a large pan. Add the gnocchi, about 40 at a time, cook until they rise to the surface and then cook for another 50–60 seconds. Remove with a slotted spoon to a large bowl and keep warm while cooking the remaining gnocchi. Repeat this procedure until all the gnocchi are done.

You can add an extra dimension to this risotto by first roasting the beetroot with some sage instead of cooking it in the stock.

risotto with broccoli & beetroot

Serves 4

Preparation time: 10 minutes

Cooking time: 35 minutes

1.5 litres vegetable stock

2 tablespoons extra virgin olive oil

4 banana shallots, finely chopped

2 garlic cloves, crushed

320 g Arborio risotto rice

250 ml white wine

salt and freshly ground black pepper

1 fresh beetroot, peeled and cut into dice

450 g broccoli, cut into 3 cm pieces

3 tablespoons chopped fresh parsley

4 tablespoons freshly grated pecorino cheese

Pour the stock into a large pan and bring to a gentle simmer.

Heat the oil in a large deep pan, add the shallots and fry gently for 5 minutes until soft. Stir in the garlic and cook for 2 minutes until it starts to soften. Add the rice and stir until the grains are glistening with butter. Add the wine and cook until it has all been absorbed.

Add a ladleful of hot stock to the rice and cook over a moderate heat for 3–5 minutes, stirring, until the liquid is absorbed. Season.

Continue adding the stock, a ladleful at a time, stirring and adding more as each batch is absorbed. The total cooking time will be about 20 minutes. About 10 minutes before the risotto is cooked, add the raw beetroot to the stock and then continue adding the stock to the rice, a ladleful at a time, as before. After another 5 minutes add the broccoli to the risotto.

When the risotto is ready, remove from the heat and stir in the parsley and pecorino. The finished risotto should be quite fluffy but not soupy. Cover and leave for 1 minute, then serve.

spelt with clams and mussels *See recipe on next page.*

In my region of Italy, Abruzzo, spelt grains are used to make risotto instead of rice. It's a very versatile ingredient and it's easy to cook.

See photograph on previous page.

spelt with clams & mussels

Serves 4
Preparation time: 20 minutes (plus soaking)
Cooking time: 15 minutes

150 g mussels
190 g clams
3 fat garlic cloves
120 ml olive oil
1 red chilli, deseeded and finely
  chopped
4 bay leaves
120 ml good white wine
400 g baby plum tomatoes, halved
  lengthways
30 g fresh basil leaves
30 g fresh flat-leaf parsley, finely
  chopped
350 g pearled spelt
salt and freshly ground black pepper
extra virgin olive oil, to drizzle

Scrub the mussels clean and remove the beards and any barnacles. Soak the clams in salted water for 30 minutes to remove the grit, then wash in clean water and drain. Discard any that have opened.

Place the unpeeled garlic cloves on a clean surface and crush with the blade of a heavy knife. Put the oil in a large non-stick frying pan and add the garlic, chilli and bay leaves. Cook for 1 minute over a low heat then remove the garlic cloves. Add the clams and mussels, cover and cook for 2–3 minutes. Once the shellfish have opened, pour in the wine and simmer for 3 minutes over a medium heat. (Discard any shellfish that remain closed.) Add the tomatoes, basil and parsley and cook for a further 5 minutes over a low heat. Set aside.

Meanwhile, bring a large pan of salted water to the boil. Add the spelt to the pan and return to a rolling boil. Stir and cook for 10 minutes until cooked. Drain.

Add the spelt to the mussels and clams, return to the heat and continue cooking for 2 more minutes. Adjust the seasoning, drizzle with a little virgin olive oil and serve immediately.

You can use most fish in a risotto but monkfish works particularly well as it is quite firm and so doesn't disappear into the rice. Tuna and swordfish would both be good substitutes.

monkfish risotto

Serves 4
Preparation time: 20 minutes
Cooking time: 35 minutes

2 tablespoons extra virgin olive oil
6 shallots, finely chopped
2 garlic cloves, crushed
350 g risotto rice
125 ml dry white wine, such as
    Trebbiano
800 g boneless monkfish, cut into
    pieces
1 litre chicken stock
1 sachet or 4–5 saffron strands
salt and freshly ground black pepper
3 tablespoons chopped fresh
    flat-leaf parsley

Heat the oil in a large deep pan and fry the shallots until soft. Add the garlic and cook for about 4 minutes. Stir the rice into the shallots, making sure each grain is glistening with oil. Add the wine and cook for 2 minutes until it has been absorbed. Add the pieces of monkfish and fry for 3 minutes.

Meanwhile, put the stock in a separate pan to simmer very gently. Add a ladleful of stock to the risotto, stirring well, and cook for 3–5 minutes until it has been absorbed. Add the saffron strands, stirring well, then continue to add the stock, a ladleful at a time. Cook until all the stock has been absorbed and the rice is al dente. This should take about 18–20 minutes. Season to taste.

Away from the heat, stir in the parsley. Cover and leave the risotto to rest for 1 minute. Serve immediately with extra freshly ground black pepper.

In Italy they eat this as a starter but I find that too heavy. It makes a fabulous light lunch or dinner, though. It's a good idea to make this soup in advance as it keeps well and the flavour improves the next day.

tuscan bean soup with pasta

Serves 4

Preparation time: 25 minutes

Cooking time: 1 hour

4 tablespoons extra virgin olive oil

350 g piece of ham or knuckle bone, thick skin trimmed

2 red onions, sliced into fine rings

1–2 garlic cloves, crushed

1 red chilli, deseeded and finely chopped (optional)

6 plum tomatoes, skinned, deseeded and chopped

1.2 litres water

675 g fresh borlotti beans, shelled, or 2 x 400 g cans borlotti beans, drained and washed

200 g macaroni

4 fresh basil leaves, torn

salt and freshly ground black pepper

freshly grated Parmesan cheese, to serve

Heat 2 tablespoons of the olive oil in a large pan and brown the ham or knuckle bone for 5 minutes, turning regularly. Add the onions, garlic, chilli (if using) and tomatoes and sauté for 3 minutes. Pour in the water and bring to the boil, skimming the surface of any scum. Simmer for 45 minutes.

Remove the ham or knuckle bone and scrape off the meat, removing the fat. Chop the meat roughly and place in a food processor with the other ingredients from the pan. Blend until smooth – this may need to be done in two batches.

Return the purée to the pan and bring back to the boil. Stir in the beans, pasta and torn basil leaves. Bring to a simmer and cook for 5–6 minutes until the pasta is tender. Stir in the remaining olive oil and adjust the seasoning if necessary.

Serve the soup with grated Parmesan to sprinkle over.

This salad is one of the many in this book that you really should try. It will fill you up while keeping you slim and healthy.

quinoa, asparagus, tomato & onion salad,
with basil and lemon dressing

Serves 4

Preparation/Cooking time: 25 minutes (plus cooling)

8 tablespoons quinoa

2 tablespoons olive oil

2 teaspoons lemon juice

2 handfuls of fresh basil, chopped

16 asparagus spears

8 vine-ripe tomatoes

2 onions

salt and freshly ground black pepper

Rinse the quinoa and drain.

Bring a pan of water to the boil, add the quinoa and simmer until tender, about 10–15 minutes. Drain and leave to cool completely.

In a small bowl mix together the olive oil, lemon juice and chopped basil. Set aside.

Peel and trim the asparagus. Blanch in boiling water and refresh in cold water.

Roughly chop the tomatoes and onions.

Place the asparagus, tomatoes, onion and quinoa in a salad bowl. Pour over the dressing and toss to combine. Season to taste.

This makes a great vegetarian main course. Or you could serve it with a grilled chicken breast – lovely.

butter bean & potato casserole

Serves 4

Preparation time: 10 minutes

Cooking time: 30 minutes

1 tablespoon olive oil

1 leek, sliced

200 g potatoes, diced

2 garlic cloves, crushed

2 x 400 g cans butter beans, rinsed
    and drained

1 glass red wine

400 g can chopped tomatoes

250 ml vegetable stock

1 bay leaf

a pinch of chilli powder

salt and freshly ground black pepper

Preheat the oven to 180°C/fan oven 160°C/Gas Mark 4.

Heat the olive oil in a flameproof casserole. Add the leek and cook over a low heat for 10 minutes before adding the potatoes, garlic and butter beans. Cook for 5 minutes then add the rest of the ingredients.

Bring to a simmer, cover and place in the oven. Cook for 15 minutes.

Remove from the oven, adjust the seasoning and discard the bay leaf before serving.

Polenta is another grain that tends to be underrated. It is quite bland on its own, but if you spice it up with a rich vegetable stew it is a fantastic food.

polenta with mixed mushrooms

Serves 8

Preparation time: 20 minutes

Cooking time: 45 minutes

1 litre water

2 teaspoons salt

175 g polenta flour

50 g butter

100 g Parmesan cheese, freshly
grated

freshly ground black pepper

5 tablespoons extra virgin olive oil

1 small onion, finely chopped

1 garlic clove, crushed

6 field mushrooms, brushed clean
and sliced

175 g wild mushrooms (porcini),
brushed clean and sliced

4 tablespoons chopped fresh
flat-leaf parsley

125 ml dry white wine, such as
Verdicchio

8 fresh basil leaves, chopped, plus
extra leaves to garnish

Put the water in a large deep pan, add the salt and bring to the boil. Reduce the heat and gradually add the polenta flour, stirring constantly with a whisk.

Simmer for 20 minutes until the polenta is very dense and separating from the side of the pan – it may seem that it has thickened faster than stated, but it really must cook on to allow the grain to become tender.

Beat the butter and Parmesan into the polenta and season to taste, adding plenty of freshly ground black pepper. Pour the wet polenta into a cake tin to form a layer about 2.5 cm thick. Spread out the mixture with a palette knife until even. Allow to set and cool.

Meanwhile, heat 3 tablespoons of the olive oil in a large frying pan. Add the onion and fry for 5 minutes until soft and just starting to brown. Stir in the garlic, mushrooms and parsley and fry for 5–8 minutes until the mushrooms are golden brown. Season. Pour in the wine and simmer for 5 minutes. Remove from the heat and stir in the chopped basil.

Cut the polenta into eight wedges and brush the tops with oil. Heat a griddle pan until very hot and place the wedges, oiled-side down on the pan, pressing them down. Cook for 2–3 minutes until golden.

Brush the uncooked side with more oil, then gently turn with a palette knife or fish slice. Cook for another 2–3 minutes until toasted. Spoon the mushroom mixture over the polenta wedges and sprinkle with torn basil leaves. Serve immediately.

You can make this dish without the black ink if you prefer. I like using it as it gives a lovely colour and flavour to the rice. Whatever you do, don't overcook the scallops!

risotto nero with scallops

Serves 4
Preparation time: 25 minutes
Cooking time: 35 minutes

1.5 litres fish stock (see page 197)
55 g butter
1 red onion, chopped
2 bay leaves
1 thyme sprig
340 g risotto rice
5 ml sachet of squid ink (optional)
150 ml white wine
16 king scallops, corals detached
    and finely chopped, washed
    and patted dry
1 roasted red pepper, deseeded and
    sliced into thin strips
2 tablespoons roughly chopped fresh
    flat-leaf parsley
6 tablespoons extra virgin olive oil
salt and freshly ground black pepper

Pour the fish stock into a large pan and bring to a gentle simmer.

Melt the butter in a large heavy-based pan, add the onion, bay leaves and thyme and cook for 3–5 minutes until the onion is soft. Add the rice and squid ink, if using, and stir for 1 minute over a medium heat. Add the wine and cook for a further 5–7 minutes until it has been absorbed.

Gradually add all but 2 ladlefuls of the stock to the rice, a ladleful at a time, stirring and adding more stock as each batch is absorbed. The total cooking time will be about 20 minutes, at the end of which the rice should be al dente. Stir in the chopped scallop corals. Set aside.

Mix the pepper strips with the chopped parsley and 4 tablespoons of the oil.

If the scallops are very thick, slice them through the middle. Heat another 1–2 tablespoons oil in a heavy-based frying pan and stir-fry the scallops for 1–2 minutes, until just tinged golden on the outside.

Return the risotto to a low heat and stir in the remaining stock. Remove and discard the bay leaves and thyme sprig. Season to taste.

Spoon the risotto onto four warmed serving plates, top with the scallops and the roasted pepper strips. Serve immediately.

This is a great way of using up leftover rice. If you have difficulty finding fresh crab you can use crayfish or prawns instead.

fried rice with crab

Serves 4

Preparation time: 10 minutes

Cooking time: 5 minutes

2 tablespoons oil

3 garlic cloves, finely chopped

½ onion, sliced

1 red chilli, deseeded (½ sliced,
    ½ finely chopped)

2 eggs

450 g cold, cooked rice

100 g fresh crab meat

1 tablespoon finely sliced fresh ginger

1 tablespoon soy sauce

1 teaspoon sugar

salt and freshly ground black pepper

2 spring onions, sliced

Heat the oil in a wok and stir-fry the garlic, onion and the chopped chilli over a medium heat until golden in colour. Move the garlic mixture to the side of the pan, then add the eggs and stir to scramble for 2 minutes. Stir in the garlic mixture, add the rice and crab, and cook for a further 2 minutes, stirring continuously.

Add the ginger, soy sauce and sugar and cook for a further 1 minute. Season. Serve topped with the sliced chilli and spring onions.

FISH

Fish is one of the foods in this book that you can eat morning, noon and night!

Growing up in a fishing village cemented my life-long love affair with fish. We ate fish almost every day. When I was a teenager and got work as a fisherman, I was paid in fish rather than money! What can be more lovely than a chilled glass of white wine with grilled sardines, drizzled with a little lemon and olive oil – it takes me back every time.

My favourite fish tend to be the oily varieties – mackerel, sardines and salmon – and you'll find plenty of these in this chapter. It never fails to amaze me that the quantities people eat here in the UK are so tiny, yet oily fish is cheap and abundant. The health benefits really are numerous – omega-3 oils have been shown to improve brain and eye function, the complexion and blood circulation. **And fish is a fantastic choice if you are on a diet – it is easily digested and low in calories.** All this, and they are sustainable too!

My preferred methods of cooking fish are grilling, baking, poaching and stewing. My favourite dressings depend on how the fish is cooked. For baked fish, I would add some rosemary and garlic; for poaching I prefer lemon, thyme and extra virgin olive oil. When barbecuing fish, don't go for the thick marinades on offer – they will simply overwhelm the delicate flavour. A dash of lime, salt and olive oil are all you need.

Fish is one of the foods in this book that you can eat morning, noon and night! **You could go for kippers in the morning, perhaps my lovely real Tuna Niçoise for lunch (see page 131), and finish with a fish stew for dinner.** After that, you will be swimming to bed!

Aldo's tips:
- **Fish is easily digested and low in calories**
- **You can eat fish morning, noon and night**
- **Don't overwhelm the delicate flavour with a thick marinade**
- **A dash of lime, salt and olive oil are all you need to barbecue fish**
- **Oily fish is cheap and abundant**
- **Omega-3 oils in oily fish improve brain and eye function, complexion and blood circulation**
- **Check that all seafood is sustainable, by looking for the Marine Stewardship Council's blue label**

Mint is normally associated with meat such as lamb but it provides an interesting fresh flavour with flat fish and is a different idea for you to try.

fillets of lemon sole with cherry tomatoes, lemon & mint

Serves 4
Preparation time: 15 minutes
Cooking time: 15 minutes

4 skinless lemon sole fillets (about 220 g each)

2 tablespoons 00 flour

3 tablespoons extra virgin olive oil

1 garlic clove, crushed

salt and freshly ground black pepper

grated rind and juice of 1 lemon

½ glass dry white wine

400 g cherry tomatoes, cut into quarters

10 mint leaves

Cut the sole fillets into long thin strips and then plait them together to make a 'braid', securing them with cocktail sticks. Cover with clingfilm and refrigerate until ready to use.

Coat the sole braids with the flour. Heat the olive oil in a pan and add the garlic. Fry briefly, then add the fish to the pan, season and add the lemon rind and juice together with the wine and leave to cook for 10 minutes. Remove the fish and set to one side on a serving dish.

Add the cherry tomatoes to the pan with the mint, check the seasoning and cook for 2–3 minutes. Pour over the fish and serve immediately.

Grouper is not widely known in the UK but in Italy it is a favourite. It is normally eaten poached or roasted as a whole fish, but I have adapted the recipe for you using fillets as it is very tasty – I urge you to try it!

grouper with wild mushrooms

Serves 4

Preparation time: 15 minutes

Cooking time: 15 minutes

4 globe artichokes

6 tablespoons extra virgin oil

240 g wild mushrooms (porcini)

½ garlic clove, finely chopped

2 fresh sage leaves

1 bunch fresh parsley, chopped

500 g grouper fillet

1 shallot, finely chopped

1 rosemary sprig

salt and freshly ground black pepper

2 tablespoons 00 flour

½ glass dry white wine

Prepare the artichokes (see page 165) and slice the hearts thinly. Heat 2 tablespoons of the olive oil in a pan and sauté the artichoke slices with some salt for 4–5 minutes. Turn off the heat but leave in the pan to keep warm.

Clean and brush the mushrooms and slice. Heat 2 tablespoons of olive oil in another pan and sauté the garlic and mushrooms with the sage over a moderate heat for 3–4 minutes. Stir in the parsley.

Cut the fish into bite-sized pieces. Heat the remaining olive oil in a third pan and sauté the shallot with the rosemary. Season the fish, toss in the flour and add to the shallot pan. Pour in the wine and cook for 4–5 minutes, turning occasionally.

Serve immediately with the artichokes and mushrooms on the side.

Fresh fish cooked simply is cooking at its best, as you get to taste the fish itself. So make sure you have really fresh fish for this dish.

monkfish with tomatoes & herbed broth

Serves 4

Preparation time: 15 minutes

Cooking time: 30 minutes

4 tablespoons extra virgin olive oil

1 small red onion, finely chopped

1 garlic clove, crushed

1 rosemary sprig

750 g monkfish

sea salt flakes and freshly ground
    black pepper

1 carrot, finely diced

2 celery stalks, trimmed and finely
    diced

350 g baby plum or cherry
    tomatoes, halved

100 ml dry white wine, such as
    sauvignon blanc

450 ml vegetable stock

3 tablespoons thyme leaves

8 sage leaves, finely chopped

Preheat the oven to 200°C/fan oven 180°C/Gas Mark 6.

Place an ovenproof pan over a low heat, heat 2 tablespoons of the oil and sauté the onion, garlic and rosemary for 5–6 minutes until soft.

Meanwhile, remove the thin film from around the fish and discard the wings and fins. Remove the central bone and cut the fish into eight large pieces. Season with sea salt and freshly ground black pepper. Add the fish to the onion mixture and cook for 3–4 minutes, turning several times.

Stir in the remaining vegetables, tomatoes and wine. Simmer for 5 minutes to reduce the wine. Add the stock and herbs and bring to the boil.

Transfer the pan to the oven and cook for 15 minutes until the fish is cooked through.

For a light lunch, spoon the fish and vegetables into the centre of four shallow bowls, then gently spoon over the broth. Drizzle over the remaining olive oil to serve.

traditional italian fish stew *See recipe on next page.*

The name 'fish stew' doesn't always appeal to people at my restaurants, which is a shame as it is a brilliant dish. There is a bit of effort involved but the result is well worth it. *See photograph on previous page.*

traditional italian fish stew

Serves 4

Preparation time: 25 minutes (plus soaking)

Cooking time: 45 minutes

340 g mussels

340 g clams

210 ml water

4 langoustines

8 raw jumbo prawns

675 g red mullet, cleaned and filleted (ask the fishmonger for the bones)

crusty bread, to serve

Stew base

3 tablespoons extra virgin olive oil

4 garlic cloves, chopped

3 thyme sprigs

2 bay leaves, torn

1 strip of orange rind

1 large onion, chopped

125 mg sachet saffron powder or a good pinch of saffron strands

2 small dried chillies, crushed

1 celery stalk, chopped

2 baby fennel bulbs, chopped

½ yellow pepper, deseeded and chopped

2 carrots, chopped

red mullet bones

1 beef tomato, roughly chopped

150 ml dry white wine

600 ml water

salt and freshly ground black pepper

Scrub the mussels clean and remove the beards and any barnacles. Soak the clams in salted water for 30 minutes to remove the grit, then wash in clean water and drain. Discard any that have opened.

To make the stew base, heat the oil in a large heavy-based deep pan and add the garlic, thyme, bay leaves and orange rind. Cook for 30 seconds, then add the onion. Cover and cook for 5 minutes until the onion softens. Stir in the saffron, chillies, celery, fennel and yellow pepper. Cover and cook for a further 3 minutes. Add the carrots, cover and cook for a further 5 minutes.

Roughly cut up the fish bones and add to the pan. Reduce the heat and mash the bones with a wooden spoon. Add the tomato and wine, increase the heat to high and boil for 3 minutes. Pour 600 ml water into the pan, bring to the boil and cook for 5 minutes. Remove and discard the thyme sprigs, bay leaves and orange rind.

Working in batches, process the stew base in a food processor, then pass it through a fine sieve and return it to the pan. Season to taste. Set aside.

Place the mussels and 60 ml water in a large heavy-based deep pan. Cover tightly and cook over a high heat for 3–5 minutes, shaking the pan frequently, until the shells have opened. Using a slotted spoon, transfer the mussels to a large bowl. Add the clams to the pan, cover and cook for 3–5 minutes until opened. Add the clams to the mussels. Add the langoustines and prawns to the pan, cover and cook for 3 minutes until bright pink. Drain and place the langoustines and prawns in the pan with the stew base.

Add 150 ml water to the fish pan juices and bring to the boil. Gently add the red mullet fillets and poach for 3 minutes until just tender. Lift the fish out and set aside. Boil the pan juices for 2 minutes, then strain and add to the stew.

Discard any mussels and clams that have remained closed, then remove the shells of half of them. Add the shelled mussels and clams to the stew. Pile the remaining mussels and clams in a large serving bowl and top with the poached fish. Reheat the stew and ladle over the fish, arranging the prawns and langoustines in the bowl. Serve immediately with some crusty bread.

Cod is the traditional choice for fish and chips but this is a lighter way to cook it. So no more deep frying! Mackerel makes a tasty and cheaper alternative.

baked cod with black olive crust & lentils

Serves 4

Preparation time: 15 minutes

Cooking time: 40 minutes

100 ml extra virgin olive oil

1 carrot, diced

1 celery stalk, diced

1 onion, diced

500 g Puy lentils

2 bay leaves

1.5 litres vegetable stock

1 tablespoon breadcrumbs

1 teaspoon fresh rosemary

1 teaspoon fresh thyme

100 g black olives

4 cod fillets (about 180 g each)

Heat half the oil in a large pan and add the diced vegetables. Cook until soft, about 3–4 minutes, stirring to ensure they don't stick. Add the lentils and bay leaves, stir a couple of times, then add the stock and cook gently until it has been absorbed by the lentils, about 30 minutes. Keep warm.

Preheat the oven to 180°C/fan oven 160°C/Gas Mark 4.

In a food processor blend the remaining oil, the breadcrumbs, herbs and black olives until you have a smooth mix.

Place the cod in a roasting tray and divide the olive mixture between the fillets, pressing it down with your fingers over the top and making sure you have an even distribution of the mix. Bake in the oven for 7–8 minutes. Serve the fish on top of the lentils.

squid & prawn skewers with aubergines and pepper salsa

See recipe on next page.

Just remember that squid and prawns must not be cooked for too long as they will become rubbery. It's a good idea to marinate the squid in milk for a few hours beforehand to make it more tender. *See photograph on previous page.*

squid & prawn skewers with aubergines and roast pepper salsa

Serves 4

Preparation time: 1 hour 15 minutes (plus marinating)

Cooking time: 35 minutes

16 raw tiger prawns, peeled and
    heads removed

2 cleaned fresh squid tubes, opened
    out and cut into large chunks

sea salt and freshly ground black
    pepper

1 tablespoon extra virgin olive oil

juice of 2 lemons

Grilled aubergines

2 aubergines

olive oil

3 garlic cloves, finely sliced

1 chilli, deseeded and finely sliced

3 tablespoons chopped fresh
    flat-leaf parsley

2 rosemary sprigs

100 ml extra virgin olive oil

Roast pepper salsa

4 red peppers

2 canned anchovies

1 small bunch fresh basil

½ tablespoon extra virgin olive oil

Slice the aubergines into 1 cm rounds, place in a colander over a bowl and add some sea salt. Leave to stand for at least an hour – the salt will remove the bitterness and excess water – then drain and pat dry.

Brush a griddle pan with a little olive oil and chargrill the aubergines over high heat on both sides. Place in a flat dish and sprinkle with the garlic, chilli, parsley and leaves from the rosemary sprigs. Pour over the olive oil and marinate for at least 2 hours.

For the salsa, sprinkle some sea salt over the peppers and roast in an oven preheated to 180°C/fan oven 160°C/Gas Mark 4, or on a barbecue, for 30 minutes, continually turning them. Remove and immediately place in a plastic bag. Tie the ends and leave to cool. When cool, peel the skin and remove the core and seeds. Place in a blender with the anchovies, basil leaves and olive oil. Blitz and set to one side.

If using bamboo skewers, soak in water to prevent burning and splintering when cooking. Place the prawns and squid in a bowl and season. Add the olive oil and lemon juice and toss. Place two prawns and some squid on a skewer, using eight in all, and cook on the barbecue or chargrill in a griddle pan for 5 minutes, or until the prawns are pink in colour.

Serve on the marinated aubergines with the pepper salsa drizzled over the top.

Saffron from the little flower that grows in my home region of Abruzzo is quite expensive, but for the colour and flavour it releases it is worth every penny.

pan-fried seabass fillet with saffron sauce

Serves 4

Preparation time: 25 minutes

Cooking time: 50 minutes

3 tablespoons extra virgin olive oil

1 shallot, chopped

1 leek, chopped

150 g risotto rice

1 glass dry white wine

600 ml hot milk

50 g mascarpone cheese

1 sachet or 4–5 saffron strands

600 g seabass fillets

salt

30 g butter

juice of 1 lemon

Heat half the olive oil in a large frying pan and cook the shallot and leek for a few minutes. Add the rice and cook for 1 minute before adding the white wine. As soon as the wine has evaporated add the hot milk and leave it to cook for 30 minutes.

In a blender, mix together the mascarpone and saffron.

Preheat the oven to 190°C/fan oven 170°C/Gas Mark 5. Heat the remaining oil in an ovenproof pan. Season the seabass fillets with salt and brown on both sides, skin-side first. Add the butter and lemon juice to the pan and place in the oven to finish cooking, about 15 minutes.

Serve the bass on top of the rice, with a dollop of saffron mascarpone on the side.

Brill is another great flat fish that is quite underrated. It's fantastic roasted, as here, or simply poached in a Court Bouillon (see page 203) – just adapt the recipe to suit yourself. Either plaice or sole could be used instead of brill.

Mediterranean-style brill

Serves 4

Preparation time: 10 minutes

Cooking time: 25 minutes

4 brill (about 300 g each), cleaned

4 garlic cloves

70 ml extra virgin olive oil

100 g black olives, stoned

400 g cherry tomatoes

2 tablespoons chopped fresh basil

4 fresh anchovies in oil

1 tablespoon capers

75 ml white wine

1 tablespoon chopped fresh parsley,
   to garnish

Preheat the oven to 190°C/fan oven 170°C/Gas Mark 5. Rinse the fish under cold running water and, with a sharp knife, slash the skin a few times on both sides.

Place the fish in a roasting dish with all the ingredients except the wine, parsley and 1 tablespoon of the basil and cook in the oven for 15 minutes. Add the white wine to the roasting dish and cook for a further 10 minutes.

Serve sprinkled with fresh parsley and the remaining basil.

Fresh tuna is both versatile and delicious. You can eat it raw or in a pasta sauce or just grilled on a salad as here – simple but effective. Yellow fin tuna is the best choice for this recipe.

tuna niçoise

Serves 4

Preparation time: 10 minutes

Cooking time: 22 minutes

8 plum tomatoes

4 soft-boiled quail eggs, peeled

1 tablespoon olive oil

4 tuna steaks (size according to
    taste)

250 g mixed salad leaves

light dressing (for example Lemon
    Dressing, page 203)

100 g French beans, blanched

2 tablespoons baby capers in
    vinegar

a handful of black olives, stoned

4 small Jersey Royal potatoes,
    cooked

8 fresh anchovy fillets

Preheat the oven to 180°C/fan oven 160°C/Gas Mark 4. Cut the tomatoes in half, place them in a baking dish and slowly roast them for about 20 minutes. Set aside.

Cut the quail eggs in half.

Brush a griddle pan with the olive oil, heat, and fry the tuna steaks for about 1 minute each side. Tuna is best when served rare, but if you like your tuna cooked through then cook for 3 minutes each side.

Arrange the salad leaves on a plate and toss in a light dressing. Arrange the beans, tomatoes, halved eggs, capers, olives, potatoes and anchovies on the leaves. Rest the tuna on top and serve immediately.

When you barbecue fish this way it absorbs a lovely smoky flavour; the only thing to watch out for is that you wet the paper enough so that it doesn't burn.

seabass wrapped in newspaper with
warm fennel & potato salad

Serves 4

Preparation time: 15 minutes

Cooking time: 20 minutes

4 thyme sprigs

2 garlic cloves, sliced in half

4 seabass (about 500 g each) or

    1 large fish (about 3 kg)

1 tablespoon extra virgin olive oil

3 tablespoons lemon juice

salt and freshly ground black pepper

lemon wedges and chopped fresh

    parsley, to garnish

Fennel and potato salad

2 medium fennel bulbs

50 g butter

a shot of sambucca

10 new potatoes, cut in half and

    cooked

1 tablespoon chopped fresh mint

Place the thyme and halved garlic cloves inside the seabass, brush with olive oil and sprinkle with lemon juice. Season with salt and pepper.

Soak some sheets of newspaper and one brown paper bag or some greaseproof paper for each fish for a few minutes, then place each fish in the bag or paper (to prevent the newsprint touching the food) and double wrap in newspaper. Cook on the barbecue for 20 minutes, turning occasionally.

Meanwhile, slice the fennel into 1 cm pieces. Melt the butter in a pan and cook the fennel for 3 minutes then add the sambucca and continue cooking for a further minute. Add the potatoes and mint and cook for 2 minutes more. Season to taste.

Remove the fish parcels from the barbecue and pull the paper off the fish – the skin will come off with the paper leaving you with just the flesh. Serve on the warm fennel and potato salad, finished with a drizzle of extra virgin olive oil and garnished with lemon wedges and chopped parsley.

ginger baked salmon   *See recipe on next page.*

Ginger is a cleansing and energizing ingredient and is one of my favourite flavours. I use root ginger to make a tea, and even juice it with apple and strawberries, and with fish like salmon it is fantastic. *See photograph on previous page.*

ginger baked salmon

Serves 4

Preparation time: 10 minutes (plus marinating)

Cooking time: 10 minutes

4 salmon portions (about 180 g each)

50 ml olive oil

200 g soba noodles, blanched for

    3 minutes

120 g pak choi

Marinade

zest and juice of 1 lemon

zest and juice of 1 lime

50 g ground ginger

50 g fresh ginger, peeled and roughly

    chopped

1 whole large red chilli

2 garlic cloves

1 lemon grass stalk

2 spring onions

200 ml soy sauce

50 ml sesame oil

3 tablespoons Thai fish sauce

    (nam pla)

1 star anise

Place the salmon portions in a dish. Blitz all the marinade ingredients, apart from the star anise, together in a blender for 3 minutes until smooth. Pass through a sieve and pour over the salmon to cover. Add the star anise. Leave for at least 4 hours but preferably overnight.

Preheat the oven to 200°C/fan oven 180°C/Gas Mark 6.

Heat half the olive oil in an ovenproof pan and fry the salmon skin-side down only for about 30 seconds (no need to season as the marinade provides that). Remove from the heat and place in the oven for 2–3 minutes.

Pan fry the blanched noodles in the remaining oil until slightly crispy. Blanch the pak choi for 5 minutes and drain.

Arrange the noodles and pak choi on serving plates and place the salmon on top.

You can use ordinary milk with this recipe as long as you add lots of fresh herbs to it, but really if you like coconut this is the best way.

wild salmon fillet with coconut milk

Serves 4

Preparation time: 5 minutes

Cooking time: 20 minutes

1 teaspoon grated fresh ginger

1 chilli, deseeded and finely chopped

1 teaspoon chopped fresh coriander, plus extra to garnish

1 teaspoon finely chopped lemon grass

1 bunch spring onions, finely chopped

200 ml coconut milk

½ teaspoon Thai fish sauce (nam pla)

a pinch of brown sugar

4 large wild salmon fillets (about 200 g each)

Preheat the oven to 180°C/fan oven 160°C/Gas Mark 4.

Place the ginger, chilli, herbs, spring onions, coconut milk, fish sauce and sugar in a bowl and mix together for 2 minutes.

Take four large pieces of foil and place a salmon fillet in each. Raise the edges of the foil around the salmon and divide the coconut milk mixture between the four 'parcels'. Close up the parcels and cook in the oven for 20 minutes.

Remove the fish from the oven and the foil. Place on a serving plate with the cooking liquor poured over. Sprinkle with more chopped coriander and serve with some steamed pak choi.

This recipe is not part of my normal traditional Italian repertoire, but I love experimenting with fish and I found this one both tasty and easy to make.

spicy squid, tiger prawn & scallop curry

Serves 4

Preparation time: 20 minutes

Cooking time: 25 minutes

1 tablespoon chopped red chilli, plus
    extra to garnish

1 teaspoon ground cumin

1 tablespoon chopped fresh
    coriander, plus extra to garnish

2 garlic cloves, crushed

1 onion, finely chopped

5 tablespoons finely chopped
    lemon grass

1 teaspoon grated ginger

2 tablespoons finely chopped peanuts

1 teaspoon tomato ketchup

600 ml coconut milk

200 g green beans, trimmed and cut
    in half

300 g raw tiger prawns, peeled

300 g squid rings, cleaned

400 g scallops, cleaned

In a processor blend the chilli, cumin, coriander, garlic, onion, lemon grass, ginger, peanuts, ketchup and coconut milk until you have a smooth paste.

Put the paste in a large pan and cook over a high heat. Once it has come to the boil, reduce the temperature and simmer for 15 minutes.

Add the green beans, prawns, squid and scallops and bring back to the boil. Once boiling, reduce the heat and simmer for 7 minutes. Serve with some chopped coriander and chillies scattered over.

I ate this dish a lot when I was doing Celebrity Fit Club. It's very healthy, it's filling and, best of all, it tastes good. It's very important that you enjoy what you are eating while trying to keep fit!

cod with pesto & aubergine houmous

Serves 4

Preparation time: 20 minutes

Cooking time: 35 minutes

12 cherry tomatoes, halved

2 leeks, roughly sliced

1 celeriac, peeled, parboiled and
    roughly chopped

4 cod fillets (about 150 g each)

1 glass dry white wine

Pesto dressing

40 fresh basil leaves

3 garlic cloves, crushed

25 g pine nuts, toasted

25 g Parmesan cheese

25 g pecorino cheese

4 tablespoons extra virgin olive oil

salt and freshly ground black pepper

Aubergine houmous

1 aubergine

400 g can chickpeas, drained and
    rinsed

3 garlic cloves

½ red chilli, deseeded

1 bunch fresh coriander

6 tablespoons extra virgin olive oil

Preheat the oven to 180°C/fan oven 160°C/Gas Mark 4.

To make the pesto dressing, rinse the basil leaves then dry thoroughly on kitchen paper. Place the basil, garlic, pine nuts and cheeses in a food processor and blitz for 30 seconds. Keep the motor running and slowly add the olive oil until all is combined. Season to taste.

To make the houmous, place the aubergine in a baking tray and roast for 20 minutes until soft. Cut in half and scoop out the flesh into a food processor. Add the chickpeas, garlic, chilli and coriander and blitz for 1 minute. Then, with the machine running, slowly add the olive oil in a steady stream.

Increase the oven temperature to 190°C/fan oven 170°C/Gas Mark 5. Scatter the vegetables over the bottom of a roasting tray, place the fish on top and pour over the white wine. Cook in the oven for 15 minutes. Serve with the pesto dressing drizzled over the top and the aubergine houmous on the side.

MEAT

...game & poultry

With meat, you need to watch the quantity and the method of cooking. You should not exceed a portion bigger than your left fist.

When using meat, always try to go for a lean cut; go for game wherever possible, as it is so much better for you nutritionally. I love wild rabbit, ostrich and venison, and you will find all of these meats in this chapter. Meat does have some excellent health benefits; it is particularly good for providing iron and essential amino acids. What you need to watch is the quantity – you should not exceed a portion bigger than your left fist - and the method of cooking. There are plenty of ways to cook meat that will retain flavour whilst reducing your fat intake. **My favourite cooking methods are similar to those I use for fish; grilling, barbecuing, baking, boiling and roasting are all good.**

You should also try to limit your intake of meat to once or twice a week and to eat it at lunch rather than supper – giving your body time to start digesting it. **Remember to always have your meat with lots of lovely seasonal veg!**

Some of my favourite recipes are the classics. I have taken a real Italian staple, Ossobuco, and given it my own twist (see page 156). Those of you who don't eat red meat at all can enjoy my lovely chicken and rabbit dishes.

Aldo's tips:

- Always go for a lean cut of meat
- Go for game, wherever possible
- Watch the quantity – do not exceed a portion bigger than your left fist
- Eat meat only once or twice a week
- Eat it at lunch rather than supper, to give the body time to start digesting it
- Always eat meat with lovely seasonal veg

My lovely mamma used to cook this dish as a luxury once a week, normally for Sunday lunch. I really recommend it! If you are not a fan of rabbit, use chicken instead.

roast rabbit mamma mia style

Serves 4

Preparation time: 20 minutes

Cooking time: 50 minutes

2 rosemary sprigs, leaves finely
    chopped

2 tablespoons chopped fresh thyme

2 garlic cloves, crushed

4 tablespoons extra virgin olive oil

sea salt and freshly ground black
    pepper

1 rabbit (about 1.2 kg), cut into
    quarters

300 ml white wine

4 large King Edward potatoes,
    peeled, quartered and parboiled

2 yellow peppers, deseeded and
    roughly chopped

Preheat the oven to 180°C/fan oven 160°C/Gas Mark 4.

Mix all the herbs and garlic with 2 tablespoons of the oil and season with salt and pepper. Rub the rabbit quarters with the herb mix, making sure you get a nice even coating.

Heat the remaining oil in a large pan. Add the rabbit and fry for 2 minutes on each side until golden brown. Transfer to a large roasting tin. Add the wine to the pan juices and bring to the boil. Boil for 3 minutes then pour over the rabbit. Add the potatoes and peppers to the roasting pan.

Roast the rabbit for 40 minutes until cooked through and tender. Serve immediately with the cooking juices spooned over the top.

Rabbit is used a lot in the south of Italy, but most often in stews, so this recipe is quite unusual. As a meat, rabbit is very good as it is quite lean.

herb-filled saddle of rabbit with courgettes

Serves 4
Preparation time: 20 minutes (plus standing)
Cooking time: 15 minutes

2 large courgettes

salt and freshly ground black pepper

4 tablespoons olive oil

1 tablespoon finely chopped fresh rosemary

1 teaspoon finely chopped fresh thyme

1 garlic clove, finely chopped

1 boneless saddle of rabbit

Using a potato peeler, slice the courgettes into ribbons. Sprinkle with a little salt and leave in a colander for 20 minutes. Rinse with cold water then pat dry on kitchen paper.

Preheat a griddle until smoking. Add some of the oil and heat. In batches, place the courgette ribbons on the griddle and cook for 1–2 minutes on each side.

Mix the herbs, garlic and 1 tablespoon of the olive oil. Season.

You will get two loins and two small fillets from the saddle. Lay the rabbit loins on a board and spread with the herb mixture. Top with the fillets and roll lengthwise. Arrange the griddled courgette ribbons on another board so they are slightly overlapping. Place the rolled rabbit on top and fold over the courgettes to form 2 parcels.

Seal all over on the griddle, adding extra oil if necessary.

Preheat the grill to medium hot. Place the wrapped meat on a foil-lined grill pan. Grill for 7–8 minutes until cooked. Remove and leave to rest for 2 minutes before serving cut into slices.

This is a really tasty easy recipe which demonstrates that if you are going to eat meat you don't have to cover it in sauces. Just go for a good cut and barbecue or grill.

marinated lamb steaks

Serves 4

Preparation time: 10 minutes (plus marinating)

Cooking time: 10 minutes

4 lamb steaks (about 200 g each;
    with bone if possible)

1 rosemary sprig

1 garlic clove

40 g sun-dried tomatoes in oil

4 tablespoons extra virgin olive oil

1 teaspoon tomato purée

350 g cooked beetroot

salt and freshly ground black pepper

1 yellow pepper, deseeded and
    roughly chopped

1 red pepper, deseeded and roughly
    chopped

1 small red onion, roughly chopped

1 courgette, roughly chopped

Put the lamb steaks in a non-metallic dish. Strip the leaves from the rosemary sprig. Place the garlic, sun-dried tomatoes, rosemary leaves, 3 tablespoons of the olive oil and the tomato purée in a food processor and blitz until smooth. Pour the marinade over the lamb steaks and leave for 2 hours.

Cut the beetroot into bite-sized wedges and put in a bowl with some seasoning and 1 tablespoon extra virgin olive oil.

Remove the lamb from the marinade and pan fry in its own juices for 3 minutes each side. Remove from the pan and leave to rest.

Add some of the marinade to the lamb pan and stir-fry the peppers, onion and courgette for 4 minutes.

Pour any juice from the lamb into the beetroot. Serve the lamb on top of the vegetables, topped with the beetroot.

grilled rump steak paillard with radicchio

I love this very simple recipe. It can be adapted to chicken, veal or lamb and will work just as well. *See photograph on previous page.*

grilled rump steak paillard with radicchio

Serves 4
Preparation time: 10 minutes
Cooking time: 10 minutes

2 heads Treviso radicchio
5 tablespoons extra virgin olive oil
2 lemons
4 rump steaks (about 200 g each)
sea salt flakes and freshly ground
    black pepper
1 tablespoon chopped fresh
    flat-leaf parsley

Preheat a griddle pan until smoking. Cut each head of radicchio into four wedges. Drizzle over 2 tablespoons olive oil and the juice from half a lemon. Griddle for 2 minutes on each side. Remove and drizzle over another tablespoon of olive oil.

Quarter the remaining whole lemon and griddle for 1 minute on each side. Set aside.

Put the steaks between sheets of clingfilm and bash with a rolling pin until very flat. Season and rub with a little bit of the remaining oil. Griddle the steaks for 1 minute on each side. Roll the steaks up.

Mix together the remaining olive oil, juice from the remaining half lemon and the parsley. Put the steaks in the centre of warmed serving plates, top each with two wedges of radicchio and spoon over some of the dressing. Drizzle the remaining dressing around the steaks. Serve with the grilled lemon quarters.

I love using lamb with fish. At Zilli Fish we have lamb and prawns, and it's a great seller. Don't panic about the anchovies in this recipe – they are really used to season the dish.

lamb chops with tomato & anchovies

Serves 4
Preparation time: 10 minutes (plus cooling and marinating)
Cooking time: 12 minutes

12 tablespoons extra virgin olive oil
3 garlic cloves, crushed
2 red chillies, deseeded and chopped
2 rosemary sprigs
1 teaspoon oregano
12 lamb chops
a knob of unsalted butter
300 g cherry tomatoes, halved
2 anchovies, finely chopped
1 teaspoon freshly ground black
    pepper
1 glass good dry white wine
1 small bunch fresh flat-leaf parsley,
    finely chopped

For the marinade, heat the olive oil in a pan with half the garlic, chilli, rosemary and oregano (do not allow it to boil). Remove from the heat and leave to cool completely. Once cool, transfer to a bowl and add the lamb chops, tossing a few times to make sure the lamb is coated. Leave to marinate for at least 2 hours.

Heat some of the marinade oil in a frying pan. Remove the chops from the marinade and fry for 3 minutes on each side. Remove the lamb from the pan and set to one side.

Add the butter to the lamb pan and then add the remaining garlic, chilli, rosemary and oregano, together with the cherry tomatoes, anchovies and pepper. When foaming, add the white wine and chopped parsley and reduce by half. Return the lamb to the pan and cook for 1 more minute, turning the chops occasionally.

Serve the chops with rosemary potatoes and the remaining cooking liquid poured over.

Ostrich meat is incredibly lean and very good for you. The taste is hard to describe, but it's a bit like lean beef. If you can get hold of some, use it instead of other meat in any recipe that doesn't involve long cooking – you will be surprised. Tortillas are great in that they can be eaten hot or cold, so you can make them when it suits you and use them when you want. The recipe below will give you more than you need to go with the ostrich fillet, just use what's left for breakfast or with salad for a light lunch.

grilled ostrich with tortilla

Serves 4
Preparation time: 15 minutes
Cooking time: 55 minutes

500 g ostrich fillet
1 garlic clove, crushed (optional)
2 tablespoons olive oil

Tortilla
800 g Maris Piper potatoes, peeled
  and cut into 1 cm thick slices
sea salt and freshly ground black
  pepper
olive oil
1 onion, sliced
6 eggs

To make the tortilla, place the potatoes in a colander and sprinkle with sea salt. Leave for 15 minutes to remove excess water. Pat dry with kitchen paper.

Put enough olive oil in a deep frying pan to come halfway up the side, and heat until very hot. Add the potatoes, turn the heat to medium. Cook for 15 minutes, add the onion. Cook for a further 15 minutes.

Whisk the eggs in a large bowl with some salt and pepper.

Drain the potatoes and onion, reserving the cooking liquid. Mix together the eggs and potatoes. Pour back into the frying pan enough of the reserved cooking olive oil to cover the base, add the potato mixture and cook over a medium heat for 10 minutes. Using a plate to invert the tortilla, turn it over and cook the other side for a further 10 minutes. Serve either hot or cold.

When ready to eat, pound the ostrich fillet lightly with a mallet and season on both sides with salt, pepper and garlic, if using. Heat the olive oil in a pan and cook for 2 minutes on each side over medium-hot heat. Rest for 1 minute before eating.

Duck meat is difficult to combine with other meats but I find this recipe with Parma ham works well. If you prefer, you can make a duck ragout instead, using the pasta sauce on page 199.

roast duck with parma ham

Serves 4

Preparation time: 15 minutes

Cooking time: 1 hour 50 minutes

2 thick slices bread

125 ml milk

1 teaspoon salt

1 duck (about 2 kg)

6 thick slices Parma ham

2 garlic cloves, crushed

120 g minced pork

120 g minced veal

2 shallots, finely chopped

2 tablespoons grated Parmesan
    cheese

1 tablespoon chopped fresh parsley

1 egg

freshly ground black pepper

75 ml olive oil

60 g butter

2 rosemary sprigs

4 tablespoons brandy

250 ml chicken stock

3 tablespoons double cream

Preheat the oven to 220°C/fan oven 200°C/Gas Mark 7. Soak the bread in the milk.

Remove any excess skin from the duck and prick all over. Add the salt to a large saucepan of water and bring to the boil. Add the duck and cook for 12 minutes. Remove and place in a colander to drain. Dry well with kitchen paper.

Finely chop two slices of the Parma ham and mix with the garlic, pork, veal, shallots, Parmesan and parsley. Squeeze the bread dry and add to the mixture, then add the egg, mix thoroughly, and season. Use the mixture to stuff the duck, then truss tightly.

Put the olive oil, butter and rosemary in a roasting tin and heat for 4 minutes. Place the duck in the middle, breast-side up, and roast for 10 minutes. Baste with the pan juices, then arrange the remaining Parma ham over the top. Reduce the oven temperature to 190°C/fan oven 170°C/Gas Mark 5 and cook for a further hour, basting regularly. Remove the Parma ham, increase the temperature to 200°C/fan oven 180°C/Gas Mark 6 and cook for a further 10 minutes. Remove from the oven and leave the duck to rest for 10 minutes.

Meanwhile, remove the duck fat from the roasting tin, leaving only juices. Place over a high heat and add the brandy. Cook until almost all evaporated then add the stock and cook until thickened. Add the cream, season, and serve with the carved duck.

Another classic Italian dish made with quite an inexpensive cut of meat – veal knuckle. Cook it long enough and it will be the tastiest meat you will have eaten in a long time.

ossobuco my way

Serves 4

Preparation time: 15 minutes

Cooking time: 1 hour 10 minutes

8 tablespoons olive oil

3 shallots or ½ large onion, finely chopped

1 chilli, deseeded and diced

4 garlic cloves, finely chopped

4 celery stalks, diced

4 large carrots, diced

100 g plain flour, seasoned

4 pieces ossobuco (veal knuckles)

200 ml dry white wine

2 x 400 g cans of chopped tomatoes

600 ml meat stock

1 rosemary sprig

4 bay leaves

salt and freshly ground black pepper

Risotto

1 tablespoon olive oil

3 shallots or ½ large onion, finely chopped

200 g risotto rice

1 glass dry white wine

1.5 litres vegetable stock

200 g peas

a knob of butter

2 pinches of saffron

100 g Parmesan cheese, grated

Preheat the oven to 180°C/fan oven 160°C/Gas mark 4.

You need to use a deep, wide, ovenproof pan. Heat the olive oil and add the shallots, chilli and garlic. Stir with a wooden spoon and add the celery and carrots. Sauté until soft.

Place the flour on a plate and roll the ossobuco in it. Place in the pan and cook for 5 minutes each side. Add the wine and simmer for 3 minutes. Add the tomatoes, meat stock, rosemary, bay leaves and seasoning and cook for a further 5 minutes. Place in the oven and cook for 40 minutes.

Meanwhile, make the risotto. Heat the olive oil in a large pan and fry the shallots. Add the rice, stirring with a wooden spoon. Add a little white wine and simmer until it is all absorbed. Start adding the vegetable stock a little at a time, making sure the rice has absorbed the liquid before adding more.

After 5 minutes add the peas, then continue adding the stock until it is all used. This should take about 25 minutes.

To finish, stir in the butter, saffron and Parmesan. Stir well and divide between four plates. Place the ossobuco on top with all the vegetables – a great Sunday lunch.

Cooking pork in milk makes the meat more tender and prevents it becoming dry. It will also make your crackling crispy.

pork braised in milk

Serves 6

Preparation time: 15 minutes

Cooking time: 1 hour 40 minutes

2.25 kg pork loin on the bone

50 ml extra virgin olive oil

4 garlic cloves, crushed

1 rosemary sprig, leaves only

salt and freshly ground black pepper

1 litre milk

zest and juice of 1 lemon

Preheat the oven to 200°C/fan oven 180°C/Gas Mark 6. Trim the bones of the ribs so that you can carve easily. Trim the fat until you are left with a thin layer.

Heat the oil in a roasting tin and add the pork. Brown all over on top of the stove, remove the meat from the tin and drain the fat away. Add the garlic and rosemary to the tin then replace the pork. Season and pour over the milk. Return the tin to the heat and bring just to boiling. Add the lemon zest and juice and transfer to the oven.

Cook for 20 minutes then reduce the temperature to 150°C/fan oven 130°C/Gas Mark 2 and cook for approximately 1 hour, depending on the thickness of the pork. Add extra milk if necessary, to make sure the meat is roasting in liquid, and baste frequently.

Remove from the oven and leave to rest before carving and serving.

I picked up this recipe on a recent trip to a Greek island and tweaked it a bit for the book. Change it how you like as it always works and always tastes sensational.

lamb stuffed with couscous & pine nuts

Serves 6

Preparation time: 15 minutes

Cooking time: 2 hours 30 minutes

3 tablespoons olive oil

1 onion, chopped, plus ½ onion

4 garlic cloves

50 g aubergine, diced

50 g courgette, diced

200 g can chopped tomatoes

a pinch of sugar

2 sprigs of thyme, leaves only

1 teaspoon capers, rinsed and dried

8 black olives, stoned and finely
    chopped

50 g couscous

100 ml boiling water

juice of ½ lemon

1 red pepper, roasted and cut into
    strips

1 yellow pepper, roasted and cut
    into strips

35 g toasted pine nuts

salt and freshly ground black pepper

1.5 kg boned leg of lamb

Preheat the oven to 230°C/fan oven 210°C/Gas Mark 8.

Heat 1 tablespoon of the olive oil in a deep pan and cook the chopped onion until soft. Add two crushed garlic cloves and cook for 2 minutes. Add 2 tablespoons olive oil, then the aubergine and courgette and cook for 10 minutes. Add the tomatoes and a pinch of sugar and cook over a low heat until thick. Remove from the heat and stir in the thyme, capers and olives.

Prepare the couscous by pouring over the boiling water and leaving for 5 minutes, occasionally fluffing with a fork. Add the lemon juice, peppers and pine nuts to the couscous. Stir the couscous mixture into the tomato sauce and season.

Fill the lamb with as much stuffing as you can, fold over, and secure with string or skewers. Put the remaining cloves of garlic on a roasting tray and add the half onion. Place the lamb on top and cook for 30 minutes. Reduce the oven temperature to 180°C/fan oven 160°C/Gas Mark 4 and cook for 1 hour. Cover the lamb with foil and cook for another 30 minutes.

Rest for 10 minutes before serving accompanied, if wished, with a cucumber and yogurt dip.

This is a classic dish from the north of Italy and is another great way of mixing meat and fish together. Give it a go, as it will really inspire your guests.

veal tonnato

Serves 4

Preparation time: 10 minutes

Cooking time: 1 hour 30 minutes (plus cooling)

1.25 kg boneless rolled veal joint

500 ml dry white wine

500 ml chicken stock

2 garlic cloves

1 onion, quartered

1 carrot, roughly chopped

1 leek, roughly chopped

2 bay leaves

3 cloves

1 teaspoon peppercorns

chopped fresh parsley and lemon
  slices, to garnish

Tonnato sauce

95 g canned tuna in oil

15 g anchovy fillets

2 egg yolks

2 tablespoons lemon juice

125 ml olive oil

Put the rolled veal in a large saucepan together with all the other ingredients, except the garnish, and add enough water to cover the veal by two-thirds. Bring to the boil, then reduce the heat and cover. Simmer for 1 hour 20 minutes until the veal is tender. Leave to cool for 30 minutes. Remove the veal from the pan and strain the cooking liquid into another pan. Bring the strained stock to the boil and cook until it is reduced to 1 glass of liquid.

To make the tonnato sauce, in a food processor blend the tuna and anchovies. Add the egg yolks and 1 tablespoon lemon juice and blend until smooth. Slowly pour in the oil, keeping the motor running, then gradually add the reduced stock until you achieve a thin mayonnaise. Add the remaining lemon juice and season well.

Thinly slice the veal and arrange on a serving platter. Spoon the sauce over and garnish with parsley and lemon slices.

Not only are ribs good food in terms of value for money, but also meat near the bone is the tastiest and quite easy and quick to cook.

barbecued pork ribs

Serves 4

Preparation time: 10 minutes (plus marinating)

Cooking time: 20 minutes

3 garlic cloves, finely chopped

1 tablespoon ground coriander

6 tablespoons muscovado sugar

1 tablespoon soy sauce

2 tablespoons olive oil

7 tablespoons ketchup

3 tablespoons oyster sauce

freshly ground black pepper

900 g pork spare ribs

Blend all the ingredients apart from the ribs together to form a smooth paste. Rub all over the pork and leave to marinate overnight.

When the barbecue is hot, lay a piece of foil over the grill. Remove the ribs from the marinade and place on top of the foil. Cook the pork, turning frequently and brushing with the marinade. Continue until the pork is cooked through, about 20 minutes – if the meat does not become charred, place directly on the barbecue for a few minutes to give it a smoky flavour.

Venison is a fantastic red meat that can be eaten raw, drizzled with a nice mustard, lemon and olive oil dressing. The following recipe is great if you are trying to lose weight, as it is a burst of protein and provides masses of energy.

thinly sliced venison fillet with bean salad

Serves 4

Preparation time: 30 minutes

Cooking time: 15 minutes

3 tablespoons olive oil

1 rosemary sprig, leaves finely chopped

1 shallot, finely chopped

juice of 1 lime

salt and freshly ground black pepper

1 whole venison fillet (about 350 g)

Bean salad

400 g can chickpeas, washed and drained

400 g can kidney beans, washed and drained

½ red onion, finely sliced

2 tomatoes, finely chopped

1 tablespoon olive oil

Preheat the oven to 220°C/fan oven 200°C/Gas Mark 7.

Put 2 tablespoons olive oil in a small pan over medium heat and stir in the rosemary, shallot and lime juice. Season and set to one side. Leave to infuse for about 30 minutes.

Heat an ovenproof frying pan, then brush the meat all over with a little of the olive oil and add it to the pan. Sear on all sides then roast in the oven for 8–10 minutes. Leave to rest for 3 minutes.

In a bowl mix together the chickpeas, kidney beans, onion and tomatoes. Add 1 tablespoon olive oil and season.

Serve the venison sliced, with the sauce poured over and the bean salad on the side.

I don't know why more restaurants don't serve baby chicken. It is a great dish and so much more flavoursome and tender than a big bird.

organic free-range lemon baby chicken
with rosemary & garlic

Serves 4

Preparation time: 20 minutes (plus marinating)

Cooking time: 45 minutes

4 organic free-range poussins (about 450 g each) or 1 large chicken, quartered

8 lemon slices

2 tablespoons black peppercorns

3 rosemary sprigs

6 garlic cloves, crushed

1 tablespoon coarse sea salt

juice of 2 lemons

4 tablespoons extra virgin olive oil

rocket and Parmesan salad, to serve

Turn each chicken over, breast-side down, and cut along just to the side of the backbone with a pair of strong kitchen scissors to open out the bird. Cut along the other side of the backbone to neaten that edge. Open out the bird, breast-side up, and press down with the ball of your hand to flatten and butterfly. This process is also known as spatchcocking. Wash the birds and pat dry on kitchen paper. Insert two lemon slices under the skin of each chicken

Next, crush the peppercorns with a pestle and mortar (or a bowl and the end of a rolling pin will do). Add the leaves from the rosemary sprigs, the garlic and sea salt and crush again. Add the lemon juice and olive oil. Rub the mixture all over the chickens, cover, and leave to marinate for 1 hour.

Cook on the barbecue for 45 minutes, turning occasionally (or roast in an oven preheated to 190°C/fan oven 170°C/Gas Mark 5). The barbecue should not be too hot as that will only burn the chicken, leaving the inside raw! Serve with a rocket and Parmesan salad.

Organic free-range is best. I don't believe in skimping when you buy food like chicken, where even the best is not that expensive.

braised chicken with artichokes

Serves 6
Preparation time: 30 minutes
Cooking time: 1 hour 5 minutes

3 globe artichokes
1 lemon, halved (zest removed and
    reserved)
1 bunch fresh flat-leaf parsley, finely
    chopped
1 garlic clove, crushed
1 red onion, thinly sliced
500 ml chicken stock
6 boneless chicken breasts
salt and freshly ground black pepper

Start by preparing the artichokes. You need to trim the stalks and peel away a few of the tough outer leaves. Using a sharp knife, cut off the tops to expose the heart. Rub the cut surfaces with a lemon half. Place the artichokes with the lemon half in a large pan of boiling water and cook for 15 minutes. Drain. Remove the hairy choke by holding the artichoke by the stalk with a clean cloth and scooping out the choke with a spoon.

Preheat the oven to 190°C/fan oven 170°C/Gas Mark 5.

Make a gremolata by mixing the parsley, lemon zest and garlic. Cover and set aside until needed.

Place the sliced onion in a roasting tin and pour in the stock. Add the chicken skin-side up. Cut the remaining lemon half in half again. Add one piece to the roasting tin and squeeze the last piece over the chicken.

Cut the prepared artichokes into quarters and add to the roasting tin.

Season and cover with foil. Cook in the oven for 20 minutes then remove the foil and cook for a further 30 minutes, until thoroughly cooked and golden brown. Scatter with the gremolata and serve.

DESSERTS

If you really can't resist dessert, I suggest you have it instead of another course. Cut out the main course, or omit the starter and have a main course followed by a dessert.

We all need a treat from time to time. I don't believe that any foods should be prohibited – life is supposed to be enjoyable. The only thing I encourage is moderation, so when you want a dessert, have one – just not every day! Try to limit your intake to once or twice a week, and at lunchtime rather than supper. If you really can't resist dessert, I suggest you replace another course with it. So maybe have just a starter and a dessert and cut out the main course, or omit the starter and have a main course followed by a dessert.

In Italy, we don't focus on desserts as much as here in the UK, where it is often seen as the most exciting course. But when we do dessert, we go for it! The desserts here range from fruit bases to sheer indulgence, such as my Chocolate Almond Muffins (see page 188) and a caffeine-free Strawberry & Orange Tiramisu (see page 186). Enjoy!

Aldo's tips:

- **No foods should be prohibited**
- **Limit desserts to once or twice a week**
- **Eat them at lunchtime rather than supper**
- **When you really want a dessert, go for it**
- **Drop another course instead, either the main course or the starter**

When making this dish make sure that the pears are quite hard to start with, so that they stay whole and don't turn into mush.

Mousse can be boring, so try spicing yours up. This is a great combination – or, for another good mousse, substitute coffee for the toffee sauce and grated chocolate for the hazelnuts.

warm pear compote

Serves 4
Preparation time: 5 minutes
Cooking time: 12 minutes

4 pears, peeled and left whole
225 g raspberries
225 g strawberries, halved
2 tablespoons brown sugar
2 tablespoons dry white wine
1 cinnamon stick
1 star anise
3 cloves

Place all the ingredients in a large saucepan and cook over a low heat until the sugar has dissolved.

Cover tightly and simmer very gently for 8 minutes or until the fruit is tender. Do not boil.

Remove and discard all the spices and serve.

banana & hazelnut mousse

Serves 4
Preparation time: 10 minutes

3 tablespoons toffee sauce
125 g crème fraîche
2 ripe bananas, roughly chopped
50 g chopped toasted hazelnuts

Mix the toffee sauce and crème fraîche together. Add the bananas and mash with a fork. Spoon into individual glasses and serve topped with toasted hazelnuts.

I've tried to create some dessert recipes that suit this great light book, and I love the combination of apricot and pistachio in this dish.

poached apricots with pistachios

Serves 4
Preparation time: 10 minutes
Cooking time: 10 minutes

125 g caster sugar
200 ml water
2 pieces orange rind, cut into
    julienne strips
2 cardamom pods
1 vanilla pod, split in half
12 apricots, halved and stoned
1 tablespoon orange juice
25 g pistachio nuts, finely chopped
Greek yogurt, to serve

Put the sugar and water in a pan and cook over a medium heat until the sugar has dissolved. Add the orange rind, cardamom and vanilla pod to the pan. Add the apricots and simmer for 7 minutes.

Remove from the heat and stir in the orange juice. Transfer to a chilled bowl and leave to cool.

Serve the apricots with a little of the syrup. Scatter over the pistachios and accompany with Greek yogurt.

I love making this recipe in the summer; it's quick, easy and very tasty. If you prefer, you can just dip uncooked bananas into the melted chocolate.

simple barbecued banana & dark chocolate mousse

Serves 4

Preparation time: 20 minutes (plus chilling)

Cooking time: 10 minutes

4 ripe bananas

225 g dark chocolate

300 ml whipping cream (whipped until firm with 1 tablespoon caster sugar)

4 scoops vanilla ice cream

2 tablespoons caster sugar

10 strawberries, sliced

After you have finished barbecuing and before you sit down to eat your meal, place the bananas (skin on) on the barbecue and let them get really black. By which stage you should have finished eating your main course.

Melt the chocolate in a container on the coolest part of the barbecue. Slip the bananas out of their skins and mix together with the chocolate.

Fold in the whipped cream and let it sit in the fridge for half an hour. Serve in sundae glasses with a ball of ice cream. Sprinkle with sugar and a few sliced strawberries.

This is a fantastic summer treat and is incredibly light and refreshing. As with most of my fruit recipes you can substitute your own favourites, but mango and passion fruit are a great combination.

passion fruit & mango sorbet

Serves 4

Preparation time: 10 minutes (plus freezing)

150 g caster sugar

250 ml water

250 ml passion fruit juice (if using
  fresh fruit, pass the pulp through
  a sieve)

3 mangoes, peeled and stoned

2 egg whites

Line a 1 kg loaf tin with clingfilm.

Put the sugar and water in a pan and warm until the sugar has dissolved. Remove from the heat and stir in the passion fruit juice.

Purée the mangoes in a food processor. Stir the mango purée into the passion fruit syrup and pour into the prepared tin. Freeze for at least 4 hours, or until set. Beat the egg whites until stiff. Remove the sorbet from the tin and blend with the egg whites. Return to the tin and place in the freezer until firm.

I am not the best at making cakes, but this one is so simple you cannot go wrong. Also in its favour – it can be made well in advance.

sugared chestnut & coffee cake

Serves 8–12

Preparation time: 10 minutes

Cooking time: 45 minutes

275 g best plain chocolate, broken
   into squares

200 g margarine

90 ml strong black coffee

25 g cocoa powder

6 eggs, separated

275 g unsweetened cooked
   chestnut purée

12 sugared chestnuts (marrons
   glacés)

icing sugar or cocoa powder, to dust

Preheat the oven to 200°C/fan oven 180°C/Gas Mark 6. Lightly grease and line the base of a 20 cm square cake tin.

Place the chocolate in a heatproof bowl with the margarine and coffee. Place over a pan of simmering water and heat gently until melted, stirring occasionally.

Place the cocoa powder in a large bowl with the egg yolks and chestnut purée. Beat until smooth. Stir the chocolate mixture into the chestnut purée mixture.

In a separate bowl whisk the egg whites until stiff, then fold into the chestnut mixture using a large metal spoon. Spoon into the prepared tin and level the surface.

Bake the cake for 30–35 minutes until it is dark brown and firm to the touch. Allow to cool in the tin for 10 minutes then turn out. Leave to cool.

Decorate with the sugared chestnuts and dust with icing sugar or cocoa powder to serve.

fruits of the forest risotto *See recipe on next page.*

Risotto is not normally served as a dessert, but this one works. You can change the fruits to include your favourites. *See photograph on previous page.*

fruits of the forest risotto

Serves 4
Preparation time: 20 minutes
Cooking time: 25–30 minutes

1 tablespoon olive oil
100 g butter
3 tablespoons brown sugar
4 tablespoons lime juice
300 g risotto rice
150 ml sweet vermouth
150 ml dessert wine
1.5 litres hot water
450 g mixed berries, such as
    raspberries, small strawberries,
    blackberries and blueberries,
    washed and drained well
25 g fresh mint, leaves only

Heat the oil in a large pan. Add 25 g butter and 2 tablespoons brown sugar. Cook gently until the sugar has melted. Stir in the lime juice.

Stir the rice into the pan and cook for 1 minute. Add the vermouth, wine and one or two ladlefuls of hot water. Add three-quarters of the berries and stir gently. Continue adding one or two ladlefuls of hot water, waiting for it to be absorbed before adding the next. It should take about 20 minutes for all the water to be absorbed.

Meanwhile, heat 25 g butter in a pan and add the remaining berries and sugar. Cook gently until the berries soften and mash into a coulis.

The risotto should be wet but not runny and the grains of rice al dente. Stir in the remaining butter and three-quarters of the mint leaves. To serve, place 2 tablespoons coulis onto each warmed serving plate, then spoon over the risotto and garnish with the remaining mint leaves.

Very naughty – but what can I say? The warm feel of this chocolate will make you feel fantastic. Every once in a while it can't hurt!

hot chocolate fondant

Serves 4
Preparation time: 15 minutes
Cooking time: 12 minutes

4 teaspoons cocoa powder
100 g good-quality dark chocolate,
  broken into pieces
100 g unsalted butter
2 eggs
2 egg yolks
120 g caster sugar
100 g plain flour

Preheat the oven to 160°C/fan oven 140°C/Gas Mark 3. Grease four ramekins about 7 cm in diameter and dust with the cocoa powder.

Place the chocolate in a bowl and set over a pan of hot water to melt. Stir continuously. When half melted add the butter and continue until the chocolate and butter are completely melted, stirring all the time. Set to one side for 10 minutes.

Whisk the whole eggs, yolks and sugar until pale and thickened then add to the chocolate mixture. Sift the flour over this and gently fold in with a metal spoon.

Divide between the prepared ramekins. Cook in the oven for 12 minutes. Remove, turn out onto serving plates and serve immediately.

I love cheesecake, especially cooked cheesecake. You could also use fresh mixed berries instead of the candied fruit.

baked honey & ricotta cheesecake

Serves 6

Preparation time: 10 minutes

Cooking time: 50 minutes

500 g ricotta cheese

5 eggs

100 ml runny honey

a pinch of cinnamon

50 g chopped candied fruit

1 tablespoon grated lemon zest

2 teaspoons marsala wine

Preheat the oven to 150°C/fan oven 130°C/Gas Mark 2.

Push the ricotta through a sieve into a bowl. Separate three of the eggs. Add the three yolks to the bowl together with the two whole eggs, the honey, cinnamon, candied fruit and grated lemon zest. Combine well. Beat the three egg whites until stiff and then fold into the mixture together with the marsala.

Pour the mixture into a greased 20 cm cake tin with a removable base and bake for about 50 minutes.

Leave to cool to room temperature then loosen using a palette knife and remove carefully from the tin.

My sister-in-law doesn't like coffee, the traditional flavouring for tiramisu, so she created this alternative last summer and I love it – so light and caffeine-free.

strawberry & orange tiramisu

Serves 6

Preparation time: 20 minutes (plus chilling)

90 ml freshly squeezed orange juice

45 ml Grand Marnier

30 sponge fingers (preferably Pavesini biscuits, available from all Italian delis)

6 egg yolks

165 g caster sugar

325 ml double cream

500 g mascarpone cheese

2 teaspoons vanilla extract

225 g strawberries, sliced

3 tablespoons icing sugar

Combine the orange juice and Grand Marnier and dip half the sponge fingers quickly in the mixture, without allowing them to soak. Arrange them over the base of a square flat dish.

In a heatproof bowl over a pan of simmering water whisk the egg yolks and the sugar until just beginning to thicken. Remove from the heat and beat until the mixture has doubled in volume and appears creamy and pale.

In a separate bowl whisk the cream until thick. Gradually add the mascarpone cheese to the beaten yolk mixture, folding it in carefully with a wooden spoon. Add the vanilla extract, then carefully fold in the cream, one third at a time.

Spoon half the mix over the soaked sponge fingers and then cover with half the strawberries. Dip the remaining sponge fingers in the orange juice mixture. Arrange half over the strawberries then cover with the remaining mascarpone mixture. Top with strawberries and finish with a final layer of sponge fingers.

Cover with clingfilm and refrigerate for 2 hours.

When ready to serve, remove the clingfilm and completely coat the top of the tiramisu with the icing sugar.

I love peaches, and prepared this way you don't have to wait until they are ripe before you can eat them.

honey peaches

Serves 4

Preparation time: 10 minutes

Cooking time: 12 minutes

4 large peaches

200 g mixed berries (blackberries, strawberries, blueberries, raspberries)

8 teaspoons lemon juice

8 teaspoons honey

mascarpone cheese

Preheat the oven to 200°C/fan oven 180°C/Gas Mark 6.

Wash and dry the peaches. Cut in half and remove the stones. Place cut-side up on a baking tray lined with foil. Fill each peach half with some berries, 1 teaspoon of the lemon juice and 1 teaspoon of the honey. Cover the tray with some more foil and bake in the oven for 12 minutes.

Remove and serve with some mascarpone and the cooking liquid spooned over.

I don't understand why people buy muffins when they are so easy to make. Try this recipe yourself and you will see what I mean. Not only do they taste good but you also get that satisfying feeling of a job well done.

chocolate & almond muffins

Makes 8

Preparation time: 15 minutes

Cooking time: 20 minutes

140 g wholemeal flour

30 g cocoa powder

1 teaspoon baking powder

½ teaspoon salt

8 tablespoons golden syrup

180 ml soy milk, with a dash of
vanilla extract

30 ml melted margarine

85 g chopped almonds, plus
8 whole almonds

Preheat the oven to 180°C/fan oven 160°C/Gas Mark 4. Grease an 8 hole muffin tin.

Whisk together the flour, cocoa, baking powder and salt. In another bowl whisk the syrup, soy milk and margarine. Add the syrup mixture to the dry mixture and stir until you achieve a smooth batter. Add the chopped almonds and stir again, being careful not to overmix the batter.

Spoon into the prepared tin, filling each hole two-thirds full. Place a whole almond on top of each muffin.

Bake in the oven for 18–20 minutes until the muffin top springs back when you press it. Serve either warm or cold.

This is a bestseller in my restaurants, and such a treat you simply have to try it. If you are having a dinner party they can be prepared in advance, allowing you to spend more time with your guests.

banana spring rolls with chocolate fondue

Serves 6

Preparation time: 10 minutes

Cooking time: 10 minutes

1 tablespoon flour

1 tablespoon water

6 spring roll pastry sheets

3 bananas, ends removed and cut
    in half

500 g dark chocolate

½ white Toblerone bar

50 g butter

600 ml double cream

vegetable oil for deep frying

Mix the flour and water together to make a paste. Lay a spring roll sheet on a board and, using a pastry brush, brush some paste around the edge. Fold into a triangle. Brush more paste around the edges and place a banana half in the triangle. Roll to make a parcel. Repeat with the remaining banana halves and spring roll sheets.

Heat some vegetable oil in a deep pan or deep-fat fryer and fry the banana rolls for about 6 minutes until brown.

Meanwhile, break the dark chocolate into pieces and roughly chop, then chop the Toblerone bar into pieces. Melt each type of chocolate in a separate heatproof bowl set over a pan of simmering water. Add half the butter to each bowl and stir until melted, then gently stir half the double cream into each. Pour the dark and white chocolate sauce into bowls.

Drain the cooked banana spring rolls on kitchen paper and serve immediately with the warm chocolate sauces.

My wife Nikki inspired this recipe as she is always bringing passion fruit home. One day it got to the point when it was a matter of binning them or cooking with them!

passion fruit brûlée

Serves 4
Preparation time: 10 minutes
Cooking time: 2 minutes

6 passion fruit, flesh removed
300 g Greek yogurt
200 g low-fat crème fraîche
1 tablespoon icing sugar
a drop of vanilla extract
2 tablespoons demerara sugar

Mix together the passion fruit flesh, yogurt, crème fraîche, icing sugar and vanilla extract then spoon into a heatproof dish.

Sprinkle over the demerara sugar and place under a hot grill for 2 minutes until bubbling and melted (or use a blowtorch if you have one).

Place in the fridge for 30 minutes before serving.

A good fish stock can be the making of a dish; a decent

lemon dressing is all you need to jazz up a plain piece of fish or

chicken. . .

These are some of the essential recipes that you will fall back on time and time again. A good Fish Stock (see page 197) can be the making of a dish, a decent Lemon Dressing (see page 203) is all you need to jazz up a plain piece of fish or chicken, and Bruschetta (see page 202) is one of those failsafe dishes that you can roll out as a starter or have for canapés – it simply cannot be beaten.

These excellent dips, dressings and sauces, together with my recipes for homemade pasta, will work for all occasions and can be used as the basis for lots of my dishes and for any of your creations at home.

Aldo's tips:
- **Make stock in large batches then chill or freeze**
- **Make a lot of pasta in one go, then freeze it**
- **Make tomato sauce in a large batch and freeze it**
- **Always use extra virgin olive oil in dressings**
- **Prevent guacamole from going brown by placing avocado stones in the dip. Discard before serving.**

Make the stock in large batches, let it cool, then chill or freeze in 300 ml bags, ready to use whenever you need it.

fish stock

Makes 1.5 litres

Preparation time: 10 minutes

Cooking time: 30 minutes

1 kg fish bones from white fish, such as sole, monkfish or turbot

2.4 litres water

1 large onion, halved

1 fennel bulb, quartered

2 celery stalks, halved

1 carrot, halved

1 leek, trimmed and quartered lengthways

8 black peppercorns

4 bay leaves

3–4 fresh flat-leaf parsley sprigs

2 thyme sprigs

Wash the fish bones, removing any traces of blood as this can make the stock bitter.

Put the fish bones, water, onion, fennel, celery, carrot, leek and peppercorns in a large deep pan. Tie the bay leaves, parsley and thyme together with a little string to make a bouquet garni and add to the pan. Bring to the boil, skimming the surface frequently with a skimming spoon to remove any impurities and fat from the stock.

Reduce the heat to a very gentle simmer and cook for a maximum of 30 minutes, continuing to skim the surface. Try to keep the vegetables and bones from disintegrating as this will make the stock cloudy.

Strain the stock through muslin and set aside to cool unless required immediately.

If you don't eat eggs, leave them out and the recipe will still work. I tend to make quite a lot of pasta in one go and then freeze it as it works just as well; cook from frozen.

basic white pasta dough

Serves 4
Preparation time: 45 minutes (plus resting)

400 g 00 flour, plus extra for dusting
5 eggs, lightly beaten
a good pinch of salt
2 tablespoons extra virgin olive oil
1–2 tablespoons cold water

Put the flour on a work surface, make a well in the centre and add the beaten eggs, salt and oil. Using your fingertips in a circular motion, slowly incorporate the flour into the egg mixture, adding water if necessary, to form a dough.

Knead for 5 minutes, adding extra flour to the surface, if necessary, until the dough is elastic and springs back when gently pressed. Cover with clingfilm and allow to rest for 30 minutes in the fridge.

I recommend that you use a pasta machine for rolling out and cutting the pasta to the desired shape. If you try to roll it out with a rolling pin it will take too long and it's unlikely that you'll be able to roll it out thinly enough.

basic spinach pasta dough
Instead of 5 eggs use 2 eggs plus 1 egg yolk. Cook 55 g spinach, drain well and purée in a blender. Add to the flour together with the eggs, salt and oil. Continue as above.

A good homemade tomato sauce is essential to any kitchen. You can use it as a base for other sauces as well as having it on its own with some pasta and Parmesan. Again, freezing is the way forward, so make a large batch.

quick tomato pasta sauce

Serves 4
Preparation time: 10 minutes
Cooking time: 35 minutes

4 tablespoons olive oil
1 small onion, finely chopped
1 garlic clove, crushed
450 g cherry tomatoes
**15 g fresh basil, torn into small
   pieces**
salt and freshly ground black pepper
**1 teaspoon soft brown sugar
   (optional)**

Heat the oil in a large deep frying pan, add the onion and cook over a very low heat for about 5 minutes, until the onion is soft but not brown.

Stir in the garlic, tomatoes and basil. Cook over a low heat for 10 minutes. As the tomatoes soften, mash gently with the back of a wooden spoon. Continue to simmer for another 20 minutes until the sauce is very thick. Season with salt and freshly ground black pepper to taste, adding a little sugar, if necessary, to balance the acidity of the tomatoes.

It is well worth making your own pizza dough as, not only do you know exactly what went into it, but you also can make it like the Italians do – with a thin crust.

pizza dough

Makes 4 pizzas

Preparation time: 30 minutes

Cooking time: 20 minutes

500 g white flour

1 tablespoon salt

15 g sachet easy-blend yeast

5 tablespoons extra virgin olive oil

150 ml warm water

Sift the flour and salt into a large bowl and stir in the yeast. Add the oil and rub it into the flour until it resembles rough breadcrumbs. Stir in the water to form a dough. Knead on a lightly floured surface for 5 minutes until quite elastic. Cover with clingfilm and leave to rest for 15 minutes.

Preheat the oven to 180°C/fan oven 160°C/Gas Mark 4.

Divide the pizza dough into four and roll each piece into a thin 15–20 cm circle. Transfer to baking trays. You may need to work in batches. Spread the top of each pizza with passata, if used, and your choice of toppings (see page 86), and cook in the oven for 20 minutes.

This salsa is fantastic with grilled fish on a hot day. For the vegetarians out there, serve it spooned over some Bruschetta (see page 202) with buffalo mozzarella as an impressive starter.

red pepper salsa

Makes 150 ml
Preparation time: 20 minutes
Cooking time: 10–15 minutes

1 large red pepper
6 tablespoons extra virgin olive oil
grated zest and juice of 1 lemon
salt and freshly ground black pepper
12 fresh basil leaves

Preheat the oven to 200°C/fan oven 180°C/Gas Mark 6.

Rub the pepper with a little oil and place on a baking tray. Roast for 10–15 minutes, turning once, until just browned and the skin blisters. Alternatively, the pepper can be charred on a ridged cast-iron grill pan (grilling on a conventional grill seems to cook peppers too much, making them too soft to peel and use in a salsa).

Allow the pepper to cool slightly, then peel the skin. Open out the pepper, catching and reserving any juices. Discard the seeds and finely slice the pepper, then dice or cut into diamond shapes. Place in the bowl with the reserved juices and stir in the remaining oil, lemon zest and juice and seasoning to taste. Tear the basil leaves and stir them into the salsa. Serve warm or cold, or store in an airtight container in the fridge for up to 3 days.

To prevent the guacamole turning brown when it is chilling, keep the stones from the avocados and place them in the dip. Remove before serving.

This is a very traditional dish in Italy and is normally topped with a red onion, tomato, garlic and basil dressing. You can use bruschetta with mussels, salads and marinated anchovies.

guacamole

Makes 150 ml
Preparation time: 10 minutes

2 ripe avocados
grated zest and juice of 1 lime
3 spring onions, trimmed and finely
**   chopped**
3 tablespoons chopped fresh
**   coriander leaves**
1 green chilli, deseeded and finely
**   diced**
salt and freshly ground black pepper

Split the avocados in half and remove the stone.

Peel the avocados, then roughly mash with a fork, but do not make the mixture too smooth. Add the lime zest and juice, spring onions, coriander and chilli. Stir to mix and season well to taste.

Add the avocado stones to the mixture and chill, covered with clingfilm, in the fridge until required.

bruschetta

Serves 4
Preparation time: 5 minutes (plus standing)
Cooking time: 4 minutes

1 round or long loaf of Italian
**   country bread**
4 garlic cloves, halved
150 ml extra virgin olive oil
salt and freshly ground black pepper

Preheat a ridged cast-iron grill pan on the hob until smoking. Cut the bread into 2.5 cm thick slices.

Toast the bread slices on the grill pan for about 2 minutes on each side. Rub the toast with the garlic and place on a large platter.

Drizzle the toast with half of the oil, breaking the surface a little to allow the oil to soak through. Season to taste. Turn the toast over and drizzle with the remaining oil. Allow the toast to sit in the oil for 10–15 minutes before serving.

This is a slightly acidic, concentrated liquid, which is used for boiling or poaching.

This is a very versatile dressing and can be used in salads, on fish or with pasta. Always make sure you use extra virgin olive oil, and you can add a little mustard for some zing.

court bouillon

Makes 1 litre
Preparation time: 10 minutes
Cooking time: 20 minutes

1.2 litres water
150 ml dry white wine
1 onion, halved
1 carrot, quartered
1 celery stalk, halved
8 black peppercorns
1 bay leaf
5–6 fresh flat-leaf parsley stalks

Put all the ingredients in a large deep pan and gently bring to the boil, skimming the surface with a skimming spoon. Reduce the heat and simmer for 20 minutes.

Strain the court bouillon through muslin and set aside to cool unless required immediately.

lemon dressing

Makes 150 ml
Preparation time: 5 minutes (plus standing)
Cooking time: 2 minutes

150 ml extra virgin olive oil
2 fat garlic cloves, crushed with
    skins still on
finely grated zest of 2 lemons
1 thyme sprig
3–4 tablespoons fresh lemon juice
1 teaspoon clear honey
salt and freshly ground black pepper

Put the oil, garlic, lemon zest and thyme in a heavy-based deep pan and heat the oil until it is hot. Remove from the heat, cover tightly and leave for 20 minutes for the flavours to infuse.

Strain the oil and add the lemon juice, honey and seasoning. Serve immediately,

CONVERSION CHART

weight

5 g	¼ oz
15 g	½ oz
20 g	¾ oz
25 g	1 oz
50 g	2 oz
75 g	3 oz
125 g	4 oz
150 g	5 oz
175 g	6 oz
200 g	7 oz
250 g	8 oz
275 g	9 oz
300 g	10 oz
325 g	11 oz
375 g	12 oz
400 g	13 oz
425 g	14 oz
475 g	15 oz
500 g	1 lb
750 g	1½ lb
1 kg	2 lb
2 kg	4 lb

measurements

5 mm	¼ inch
1 cm	½ inch
1.5 cm	¾ inch
2.5 cm	1 inch
5 cm	2 inches
7 cm	3 inches
10 cm	4 inches
15 cm	6 inches
18 cm	7 inches
20 cm	8 inches
25 cm	10 inches
30 cm	12 inches

liquids

15 ml	½ fl oz
25 ml	1 fl oz
50 ml	2 fl oz
75 ml	3 fl oz
100 ml	3½ fl oz
125 ml	4 fl oz
150 ml	(¼ pint)
175 ml	6 fl oz
200 ml	7 fl oz
250 ml	8 fl oz
275 ml	9 fl oz
300 ml	(½ pint)
325 ml	11 fl oz
350 ml	12 fl oz
400 ml	14 fl oz
425 ml	(¾ pint)
600 ml	(1 pint)
750 ml	1¼ pints
900 ml	1½ pints
1 litre	1¾ pints
1.2 litres	2 pints
1.5 litres	2½ pints
2 litres	3½ pints
2.5 litres	4 pints

oven temperatures

110°C	225°F	Gas ¼
120°C	250°F	Gas ½
140°C	275°F	Gas 1
150°C	300°F	Gas 2
160°C	325°F	Gas 3
180°C	350°F	Gas 4
190°C	372°F	Gas 5
200°C	400°F	Gas 6
220°C	425°F	Gas 7
230°C	450°F	Gas 8

dry US conversions

flour: 115 g	1 cup
butter: 225 g	1 cup
breadcrumbs (fresh): 50 g	1 cup
grated Parmesan: 115 g	1 cup
grated cheddar: 115 g	1 cup
dried fruit: 170 g	1 cup
ground nuts: 115 g	1 cup
almonds: 140 g	1 cup
walnuts: 115 g	1 cup
rice: 200 g	1 cup
sugar (caster/granulated): 225 g	1 cup
icing sugar: 115 g	1 cup

liquid US conversions

5 ml	1 teaspoon
15 ml	1 tablespoon
60 ml	¼ cup
120 ml	½ cup
180 ml	¾ cup
240 ml	1 cup
300 ml	1¼ cups
350 ml	1½ cups
400 ml	1¾ cups
475 ml	2 cups
600 ml	2½ cups
750 ml	3 cups
1 litre	4 cups